LIVE BETTER A
THROUGH PSYC

More than four million people have followed Dr. Maltz's directives toward leading fuller, more satisfying lives. Using his latest and best-documented book, you too can translate his time-tested yet still revolutionary theory into measurable action and visible improvement.

Case histories, exercises for practical application, and questions and answers to increase your understanding make this the most effective of Dr. Maltz's best-selling books.

Learn to project your strengthened self-image to your very best advantage. Banish pessimism, self-pity and inferiority feelings from your vocabulary and your life. Transform your failures into a never-ending succession of shining triumphs.

Books by Maxwell Maltz

Creative Living for Today
The Magic Power of Self-Image Psychology
Psycho-Cybernetics
Psycho-Cybernetic Principles for Creative Living
Thoughts to Live By

Published by POCKET BOOKS

Psycho-Cybernetic Principles for Creative Living

by Maxwell Maltz, M.D., F.I.C.S.

PUBLISHED BY POCKET BOOKS NEW YORK

The format for this book was derived from my Psycho-Cybernetics Workshop Books: *The Quest for Success* and *Happiness*, published in 1965. My other books consulted were: *Psycho-Cybernetics, The Conquest of Frustration, Creative Living for Today, Five Minutes to Happiness, Psycho-Cybernetics and Self-Fulfillment, Power Psycho-Cybernetics for Youth* and *The Search for Self-Respect*.

Another *Original* publication of POCKET BOOKS

POCKET BOOKS, a Simon & Schuster division of
GULF & WESTERN CORPORATION
1230 Avenue of the Americas, New York, N.Y. 10020

ISBN: 0-671-43571-X

First Pocket Books printing December, 1974

10 9 8 7 6 5

POCKET and colophon are trademarks of Simon & Schuster.

Printed in the U.S.A.

Contents

Introduction

Your life should be an adventure, an ongoing series of rich experiences, a process of setting goals and achieving fulfillment through realizing them.

Every day should bring a spiritual triumph like a warm sun bursting through the clouds.

My purpose in writing this book is to help you to penetrate the fog, disperse the clouds, and reach back into the heart of yourself and grasp firmly the inner confidence, the success orientation, the radiance, that can be so easily lost along the way.

Psycho-Cybernetics, finished in 1959, has been read by millions of people in this country, translated into many foreign languages, and digested by many more millions throughout the world.

"But," you may ask, "does psycho-cybernetics really work?"

Fifteen years after publication, the thousands upon thousands of letters and case histories submitted by readers testify to the fact that it does work. And, in this volume, principles, guidelines, and exercises will guide you toward ever richer living.

My theory of creative psycho-cybernetics has already helped enormous numbers of people to redirect their energies, to harness their constructive aggression into positive channels. It is widely applied today in industrial, educational, and religious circles.

Creative psycho-cybernetics works because it is basic.

It gets below superficial appearances to motivation and to a sense of purpose of the individual, guiding him in cutting through the confusion and complexity of modern existence to clearly defined objectives, bringing him satisfaction and genuine fulfillment.

In a sense, this is a cinematic experience, like sitting calmly at the movies and watching the feature attraction.

Is it a *tour de force,* or is it a turkey? It is up to you. This gripping production is your responsibility. You are producer and coproducer, director and stage manager, prop man and actor. You are the writer; it is your scenario. You are the audience—and the critic.

The drama that unfolds before your eyes is about—you. The story line—does it involve happiness or misery, success or failure, laughter or tears? Only you can tell. This is your creation, and you are the dominating force. Only you can call the shots.

I have high hopes that many of you will profit from this visual self-appraisal, for a powerful tool is at your side, waiting in the wings, preparing to respond on cue and to stage a scintillating performance. Without doubt, it is the caliber of your self-image that will cause you to rise to new heights or to descend to depressing depths.

You can't see or touch your self-image but it is nonetheless real. It is your picture of yourself and, false or true, this image of yourself moves you toward positive or negative experiences, and it does so every day of your life. Its crucial importance stems from the fact that your personality revolves around this conception of self. In simplified terms, if you see yourself as a fine person, you are on the road to satisfaction, achievement, and pleasure; if you see yourself as inferior and unworthy, you fail before you start.

You think you are a chronic failure? You can't do anything right? You stumble around in circles, plod wearily from defeat to disaster? And you ask, "Is there hope for me too?"

My answer is affirmative, even in this negative, cynical age. Yes, there *is* hope—if you can change the fiber of your self-image, if you can transform a gray picture that weighs down your mind into a bright sunny one.

And this is where we must focus our energies: in the playhouse, the theater, of your mind. Here is where we will work to change this vital image of yourself, struggling to turn the power of this image to constructive use, releasing you from obsessive failure pictures and bringing you into the inspiring world of possibility.

Let us begin this voyage of internal discovery, our joint objective being the search for the strong self-image that will make it possible to lead richer, fuller, happier lives. We start this journey with enthusiasm and the determination that it will fulfill its promise.

Chapter 1

Your Best Friend: Your Self-Image

The complexity of living in today's world is no secret to thinking people. Each day we are embroiled in confusion and struggle, and many people drown in the stormy sea of troubles. But others survive—and grow.

They are able to do this in spite of misfortune. The most hardy of these determined individuals reach back into themselves for something extra in times of stress. What is this something extra? It is a powerhouse, a treasure trove—it is self-image.

Sooner or later, everyone encounters conflict and defeat, even catastrophe, but are these grounds for pessimism? Absolutely not! Pessimism does not do anything for you; it negates your life force and blunts your healthy appetites. You can realistically see life's difficulties and problems without pessimism, without self-pity, without crumbling under feelings of inferiority.

Recently, I received this letter:

Dear Dr. Maltz:

Please let me express to you my feelings of gratitude for the opportunity to know of a better way to live through your book called *Psycho-Cybernetics.*

There is no doubt in my mind of the validity of your book. I was a psychology major in college and I guess, subconsciously as I read your book, I was mentally testing everything you said.

This book is written in such simple and easy-to-understand language that even a young child could understand it.

As someone with a crippling disease, muscular dystrophy, it is most important that my mind be as free and clear of negative thought and resentments as is humanly possible!

So I use *Psycho-Cybernetics* as a work manual for everyday use and at times I am sure that someone slipped in some new material when I wasn't looking.

May many others find the comfort, knowledge, and better way to live each day as I have found through knowing you and your book *Psycho-Cybernetics!*

To a Better Day,
Mrs. Peter (Jeanne) Sanders

I quote this inspiring letter so that you can view your own problems in perspective and feel motivated to rise above them. Give serious consideration to what will fortify you to face life's challenges with confidence: your image of yourself.

This woman's communication intrigued me, and I asked her if she would send me a more detailed profile. Here it is.

CASE HISTORY

Perhaps I should begin by saying that I am very grateful to be able to express my joy and a feeling of fulfillment as a whole integrated human being.

What I am about to share with you is very personal and charged with much emotion. When I think of how one paperback book has changed my whole life style and has altered the entire course of my human experience, is it any wonder that I want to tell you my story, hoping that others may know that there is a better way to live!

My life began in Providence, Kentucky, on October 1, 1924, as a lively, healthy, normal, nine-and-a-half-pound baby girl. I was stricken with muscular dystrophy at the tender age of ten.

One of my earliest recollections, which left a deep scar,

occurred shortly after the diagnosis was made. I overheard the doctor telling my parents that they might as well take me out of school as I had less than a year to live. This experience was not only painful and deeply etched with great fear, but was only one of many brutal experiences that I encountered.

Gradual changes began to take place in my motor abilities. I began to stumble more and more, and it became exceedingly difficult for me to walk. At the same time I began to experience great difficulty in the use of my hands.

With loving and understanding parents, I began a journey that was to span a period of twenty years trying to cope and adjust to this progressive, crippling shadow of doom, muscular dystrophy.

Many summers were spent in hospitals in body casts, in therapy, and in learning to walk again. Finally, specially built shoes with steel braces attached were provided to help me to walk. It was becoming more obvious every day that my whole body was showing signs of weakness.

Many days of discouragement followed. At that time, I did not know the beauty of learning to live mentally when my physical problems were so great. Tasks that were so simple for others were great frustrations to me. I spent many hours learning to tie my own shoes. Buttons and zippers are still very difficult for me.

In spite of numerous obstacles, I managed to complete my education, which included college. Then came ten years of teaching school in Michigan in the public schools and three years teaching in a government nursery school for working mothers. This government school was provided for working mothers involved in war-related work during World War II.

At the age of twenty-five, I was told that I must undergo an operation on both ankles or face spending the remainder of my life in a wheelchair.

After suffering the most excruciating ordeals of living through these operations, almost a year of confinement in casts and wheelchair and more physical therapy, I had to learn to walk again. But learning to walk involved a totally new way of moving my legs. To permit me to walk without the aid of braces, the operation had stabilized my ankle joints and fused all of these joints into one main shaft of bone.

For the first time in twenty years I was able to shed the heavy steel braces. It was many months later before I could stand for long periods of time. It was several years later before I was able to return to work.

Even though, for the most part, the operations were a success, the mental scars remained. These mental scars became a greater handicap to me than did my physical disabilities. I lacked self-confidence, self-esteem, and self-reliance and carried with me a great inferiority complex. I seemed to have lost a sense of direction and a purpose in living.

It was at this stage of my life that many well-meaning friends and my family tried to help me. Inspirational booklets, books, and a desperate search into all types of philosophy filled every waking moment. I investigated everything from Buddhism to Transcendental Meditation. I even delved into some of the Ancient Vedas.

One day while browsing in a local bookstore, my eye caught sight of a book with the title *Psycho-Cybernetics*. The name aroused my curiosity. I did not know what it meant. I was told by the clerk in the store that she simply couldn't keep enough copies on hand. She said that it was one of the best-selling books in her store. That was all I needed to hear. I bought a copy and found, as I began to read the book, that I couldn't lay it down. For the first time in my life I began to gain an insight into my own behavior. Suddenly the answers that I had been seeking were right there.

As I finished the book, I decided that someday I would meet the author, Dr. Maxwell Maltz. I didn't know how this meeting would come about, but I knew I must have the opportunity to tell Dr. Maltz of my appreciation for a new beginning to my life.

Over a period of years, *Psycho-Cybernetics* by Dr. Maxwell Maltz, world-famous plastic surgeon, has served as an action manual for me. The book describes suggested definite methods and procedures which have been used successfully in the lives of thousands of others. As in my own life, these procedures have produced the most remarkable changes. But as Dr. Maltz states in his book, each of us is responsible for his own life. The power to change lies within.

I have come to know what it is to live a more fulfilling, useful, and happy life. My attitude has changed from the negative to a "winning feeling," of confidence that I can accomplish anything my mind can conceive and believe. What appears to be a miracle to others is simply my working to change my own self-image.

I have become somewhat of a medical phenomenon. Every doctor that has examined me has said that I do not have the physical muscle ability to walk. From a medical standpoint there seems to be no logical explanation.

I was recently named "Handicapped Professional Woman of the Year" at the District 4 Pilot International Annual Convention held in St. Petersburg. This award is sponsored jointly by Pilot International and the President's Committee on Employment of the Handicapped. Pilot International is a women's classified service organization patterned after Rotary.

I have just been appointed to Governor Askew's Sub-Committee on Information and Press Relations on Employment of the Handicapped [Florida].

Through my work in television, I have had the good fortune and pleasure of working with many well-known personalities from all walks of life. Among those notables was Dr. Maltz. At last I was afforded the opportunity to express appreciation for all that *Psycho-Cybernetics* has done for me.

As Dr. Maltz states in his book, the self-image is changed, for better or worse, not by intellect alone, nor by intellectual knowledge alone, but by what he terms "experiencing." "Wittingly or unwittingly we develop our self-image by our past creative experiences." "We can change it by the same method." We are not taught love; but as we "experience" it we are in the process of growing into healthier, happier, and well-adjusted human beings. "Our present state of self-confidence and poise is the result of what we have experienced rather than what we have learned intellectually," as stated by Dr. Maltz.

I would like to close by quoting from another great mind, William James:

"The sovereign voluntary path to cheerfulness, if our spontaneous cheerfulness be lost, is to sit up cheerfully, look around cheerfully, and act and speak as if cheerfulness were already there. . . .

"If we act as if from some better feeling, the bad feeling soon silently steals away."

The above short autobiography was written with love for Dr. Maxwell Maltz and his wife Anne and may be used in any way which will bless my fellow man!

Mrs. Peter (Jeanne) Sanders

The Muscle in Your Self-Image

I quote this letter in its entirety because, in spite of obviously overwhelming physical handicaps, this remarkable woman has channeled her energies so strikingly, fulfilling her potential with such constructive application of sound principles.

Yes she can walk, and she drives a car. No muscle in her legs, and yet she walks. A miracle? No, a demonstration not of supernatural phenomena but of real muscle. Medically speaking, a muscular disability would not permit her legs to stand up to the challenge of walking, and still she was not daunted—and she walked again. With what muscles? Ah, you cannot see them, but they are part and parcel of her self-image.

Jeanne and her husband Peter are dear friends of my wife and myself today. Jeanne does not feel disadvantaged and I have never known her to submerge herself in self-pity. In truth, she is optimistic, friendly, and responsible in attitude.

A marvelous victory of mind over matter! A superb example of the healing, burning fire of mental willpower! A wonderful exhibition of the power in self-image!

Now, what about *your* self-image? Do you build its muscles each day with exercises? Do you warm it up as diligently as you would the motor of your automobile on a cold day? You may say that you have to take good care of your automobile because it takes you places. Well, friend, so does your self-image.

And now the question arises: How does one build his self-image to meet the challenges of life?

First, study my theory of creative psycho-cybernetics and comprehend the staggering power that lies in your self-image A defective self-image will damage the quality of your life in spite of splendid motivation and willpower. Indeed if your life is going poorly the root of your trouble is probably a defective self-image. But you can change this mental picture—through psycho-cybernetics. You can build a new picture of yourself.

You must understand yourself. but this does not mean digging morbidly into the past to wallow around in remorse and guilt Your past is part of what you are today. Still, if you dwell on yesterday, you will continue to be an unhappy individual today. Instead. dwell on to-day and your future. Build a new self-image to steer you toward the kind of person you wish to become. Your old behavior is built around an image to which you respond automatically. By creating a positive self-image from a negative self-image, you transform your automatic behavior from negative to positive.

17

Life has purpose and we are not on this earth by accident. With a past reaching back to stardust and a future proceeding to eternity, we must find purpose in life. Only in defining realistic goals and moving toward these goals do we establish a sense of direction that can preserve us from uselessness and emptiness. Profiting from our blunders, and using our experiences to interpret the signposts correctly, we keep heading in a worthwhile direction.

This direction is determined by the nature of our mental image of ourselves. You see, we react fundamentally to this feeling about our true value which, though subjective, has been programmed into us. Much more than many people realize, life style is predetermined by habitual reactions flowing from the self-image.

This basic self-conception leads us to be accident-prone, happiness-prone, relaxation-prone, or defeat-prone. Depending on the nature of this self-image, we respond with triggered reactions when someone presses buttons that set off our conditioned reflexes. These conditioned reflexes are based, not on reality, but on what imagination represents as reality. When our responses to reality are unreal, we antagonize others. Most people retreat fearfully from an individual with the self-image of a Napoleon.

The exciting thing is that, except in severe mental illnesses that require professional help, this all-important self-image is something we can change. For most people, psycho-cybernetics provides the tools for transforming our lives through building a new strong self-image.

And, like Jeanne Sanders—a physically handicapped, but emotionally gutsy woman—you can do it too.

Assumptions

By changing our self-image in positive ways we enrich the quality of our lives.

18

It is within our power to set realistic goals and move to achieve them.

When we discover our shortcomings, we must harness the courage to rise above them.

The internal changes in us will begin to take root when we realize the degree of control we can exercise.

These basic preconceptions do not apply to people with serious mental illnesses. Most individuals, however, in concretizing these assumptions, should be able to feel new hope for a new life.

The Method

Significantly, we differentiate between the person we are and the person we would like to become.

As a corollary to this, we realize the need to change our current behavior or our present ideals.

We formulate worthwhile goals within our innate and developed capabilities.

Consciously, we commit ourselves to these new creative goals.

The strength of the commitment will govern the speed and potency with which we advance to our goals.

Our mistakes (negative feedback) serve as aids to our relearning and further motivate us for growth.

QUESTIONS AND ANSWERS

Q. Am I a robot controlled by buttons pushed by other people? Am I a reactor instead of an actor? What is the nature of my built-in triggered responses?

A. Typical "buttons" include the following:

Politics. My party is always right. Others are always wrong or, to be charitable. misguided.

Religion. Mine is the enlightened one. Other denominations are heretical, their membership wrong-minded.

Any product I buy is a triumph of shrewd appraisal. In criticizing my purchase, you insult my intelligence. When you buy different articles, this displays your stupidity.

Yes, I buy certain brand names. Doesn't everyone realize their superiority?

What's it to you if I smoke or drink excessively?

What can one expect from an ignorant foreigner?

I have no latitude in choosing wearing apparel; I wear what's "in."

Each year I buy a new car. It's the thing to do.

Using a credit card does not seem as expensive as shelling out cash.

Drinking a particular brand of whiskey will make me a person of distinction.

I walk around ladders, avoid black cats, and carry a rabbit's foot.

For good luck, I throw coins in wishing wells. Breaking a mirror or spilling salt upsets me.

Q. What is the basic key to personality and behavior?

A. The self-image.

Q. What happens when you change this image?

A. You change your personality and behavior.

Q. And when you expand the self-image?

A. You expand the entire area of personal potential.

Q. What causes proneness to accidents, failure, and so on?

A. Negative self-image.

Q. Why is it that the "power of positive thinking" helps some individuals but not others?

A. If the self-image is defective, it will not work.

Q. Can you explain the present composition of a person's self-image?

A. It reflects creative experiencing of successes, negative experiencing of failures, and repetition in your mind of these successes or failures.

Q. How can one shape a healthier mental picture?

A. Through feeling and imaging in terms of success, and setting inspiring goals in terms of this new concept of one's self.

Q. How can one develop the habit of successful experiencing if one has not experienced the feeling of success?

A. If you can imagine success, vividly and in detail, it is real to you and can trigger off a new feeling about yourself.

Q. Why does a make-believe experience change the self-image?

A. The human nervous system is unable to distinguish between a real experience and one imagined vividly and in detail.

Q. Will the simple reading of *Psycho-Cybernetics* change my self-image?

A. No. The techniques must be lived, must be felt and responded to creatively and energetically.

HOMEWORK

More questions and answers follow; but, first, a short assignment: What does success mean to you?

This is an important concept, so take your time and organize your thinking carefully. Fortify yourself with a few sheets of paper or a scratch pad, sharpen your pencils or line up a phalanx of ballpoint pens—and go.

Respond as if this were a home-study course, with you entrenched as student and instructor—a dual role, but you must feel that you can handle it. Write the answer in detail. Your random thoughts and free associations on the meaning of success will, to a degree, translate themselves into fundamental forces shaping the development and orientation of your self-image.

A few ideas? These questions and answers are merely a general guide. You must appraise success in your own terms—otherwise, this exercise is meaningless.

Anyway, ponder these thoughts on success:

Tranquillity, contentment, sensitivity to other people.

Living vibrantly, joyfully, without unreasonable limitations on self-expression.

Think about your capacity to shed what is not important, to ward off triviality, to put aside time for self-analysis, meditation, and attention to self-fulfillment.

Consider rising above such handicaps as fear and resentment in order to reach the finest side of your personality: the self-accepting, warm, loving individual you sometimes are.

Assume an almost-egoless absorption in other people, in which you contribute to others, enriching them as you enrich yourself in the interaction.

As I said, these are just possibilities. Don't let these thoughts control your personal self-expression or inhibit the drift of your own thinking on success.

You have finished this assignment, but you probably have more questions to be answered. Let us resume our probe into the nature of the mental image that is crucial to your future welfare.

QUESTIONS AND ANSWERS

Q. Regarding our triggered reactions, when our "buttons" are pushed, how do we evade these compulsions toward overconformity?

A. By discovering and building the real self.

Q. And what is this real self?

A. The invaluable core of our personality, which is often buried under layers of defensiveness.

Q. And the self-image?

A. A mental blueprint of the kind of individual you are.

Q. What shapes this image?

A. Beliefs, including past successes and failures, reactions from other people, demands of our culture, and what we have learned from prior experiences.

Q. What is our response to this image?

A. Rarely if ever do we question its validity—no matter how untrue or irrational its components may be.

Q. What element in our life is ruled by this mental image?

A. The self-image rules our life style, controlling our feelings and actions. Our behavior is a reflection of what we think of ourself.

Q. How can we change our personality?

A. By changing our self-image. Until we do this, changes will be only temporary.

Q. Can "positive thinking" override the self-image?

A. Positive thinking is a useful tool in changing the self-image, but it will not change the personality by itself.

Q. How does one accept a new idea?

A. This will be no problem if the idea is consistent with one's present beliefs.

Q. Does the new idea produce change in us if it is not consistent with our basic convictions?

A. We reject it without changing. There is a fundamental difference between "I am a failure" and "I failed that exam." In the first case, the self-image is hopelessly weak; in the latter case, there is an objective self-image which can accept a failure and can later rise above it to enjoy future successes.

Q. What happens when someone imagines he is ugly?

A. He acts as if this were really true and feels that he is repulsive to others.

Q. Is this belief related to "I am a failure" and "I failed that exam"?

A. Yes. The person with a strong self-image can accept that he is not Rudolf Valentino, but he will still feel a pride in his imperfect appearance.

Q. What are the ingredients of a strong self-image?

A. Self-respect, belief in oneself, confidence, support-iveness.

Q. Can we tell when this image is proper?

A. When our self-conception is secure, we are able to express our views surely, function effectively, and support ourselves in spite of criticism.

Q. When is the self-image improper?

A. When the self-image is weak, we feel anxious and ashamed. We retreat from creative expression and defend ourselves with either evasion or hostility.

Q. When are we enjoying life?

A. When we expand emotionally—through joy, through self-assertion, through constructive aggression.

Q. How do we choke off emotional expansion?

A. Through inhibition and self-condemnation.

Q. Does normal human behavior include hatred, guilt, and destructiveness?

A. More to the point, it includes a strong instinct to live and to grow.

Q. How does this life instinct work?

A. Through the Creative Mechanism.

Q. What is this Creative Mechanism?

A. It is the goal-striving part of your brain and your nervous system, programmed by the mind and operating spontaneously.

Q. Is this mechanism capable of discrimination?

A. Operating impersonally, it works for or against us, depending on the nature of the goals built into our image of ourselves.

Q. What causes this mechanism to function?

A. Clear objectives.

Q. And how are objectives implanted in the mechanism?

A. Through the mental images we create.

Q. What is the most basic image a person can place in the mechanism?

A. An image of himself.

Q. What will be at the center of this image?

A. His most cherished goals.

Q. And how will the self-image bring about accomplishment of these goals?

A. By prescribing guidelines for their achievement.

Q. What kind of data does the mechanism process?

A. Our thoughts, convictions, interpretations.

Q. What if we feed the mechanism negative data?

A. The mechanism will throw out negative responses. Computer operators use a symbol "GIGO," meaning "garbage in, garbage out." Garbage inserted into a computer emerges as the same garbage. When you place "garbage" into your Creative Mechanism, it will certainly not come out smelling like roses.

Q. Can we convert this Creative Mechanism from a failure mechanism into a success mechanism?

A. Yes, by developing new positive patterns of thinking and imaging.

Q. How will this improve our way of life?

A. By leading to formation of a stronger self-image and by turning our normal creative mechanism into a success mechanism.

SUMMARY

Now, let us summarize the meat of the material discussed in this chapter.

We aim to strengthen our resolve and to enrich the quality of our lives by focusing on the basic element in personality—the self-image. This mental image is a foundation upon which you build the structure of your personality. Your concept of what you are like as a person determines the ways in which you act and shapes your objective personality.

Thus, if you can change your preconceptions and the interpretations constituting your self-image, you can change your way of life.

You become your own plastic surgeon. You remove your inner scars, and overlook external scars.

You do this by feeding positive data into your impersonal Creative Mechanism, building your self-image as a strong and healthy figure. With positive data, the Creative Mechanism, a built-in tool, will function faithfully as a success mechanism, leading you automatically toward waves of confidence and self-esteem.

Obviously, if you feed negative data into this Creative Mechanism, it will work against you instead of for you. How do you avoid this? By building a healthy self-image. With a good mental picture of yourself, you feed positive data into the automatic servomechanism, and it will function as a success mechanism.

You think you are a Doubting Thomas, a professional cynic? You are so immersed in pessimism that you deny the possibility of change? You think if an emotional change came and walloped you between the eyes you wouldn't even blink an eyelash?

Let me quote another letter, this one from Canada.

Dear Dr. Maltz:

As I mentioned to you during our brief conversation this morning after your talk on psycho-cybernetics and self-fulfillment, I do know someone whose life you saved. The individual in question had a poor self-image, had no goals, little desire, and a "heavy load" to carry. He was a father of two young sons, the normal monotonous day-to-day job with a company that offered no incentives to progress; and, to complicate matters, he had taken to smoking marijuana on a regular basis. His background was not of a poor environment; however, he did not have any guiding force to teach him about the great secret of his own mind.

He was constantly looking for "something" and had never found it. It was, I'm sure, solely because he had no idea of which direction or what tools to use to accomplish set goals. One day, about two years ago, the turning point of his life arrived. He had mortgaged his house to go into a new field, had quit his job and still had no assurance or guidance. In the presence of his wife (a childhood sweetheart) he lit a "joint" and thought perhaps depression would be overcome. To the contrary—his first reactions were an in-depth study of "the who, why, and where" syndrome. His questioning came to a point where his own existence was one big question mark. After a night of terror in which suicide seemed the only way out and no help, thanks to a kindly family physician, a restless sleep of a few short moments was had.

Upon awakening, although the effects of the drug had worn off, the experience he had had while still under the influence of the drug lasted for four months. The love of life was gone, the love of family had deteriorated to nil, and the questions of existence were now foremost in his mind: How did I get here? What am I doing here? and Why do I need it?

Family meant nothing, trees meant nothing, people meant nothing, the world meant nothing. Hell was here!!

Then he remembered your book *Psycho-Cybernetics*—and that's where it all started to come back with interest. There was a way to change your self-image—improve your self-image. There was a way to guide one's life. There was a way to *love*, there was a way to success, it was all there!! A psychiatrist couldn't help, although he tried and failed, because he did not know that all this man needed was a better opinion of himself in the present, goals for the present and the future and not a study of the past.

To sum up (I did intend to be brief): The success this man had in his life, through building a satisfactory self-image, through building realistic goals and guiding his own mind, is solely the responsibility of one Dr. Maxwell Maltz and his book. He has since gone on to become successful in his ever-growing business of weight reduction and self-fulfillment and is now entered in the race for alderman in his area in Canada. He is twenty-nine and has a staff of forty in his enterprise. His name is C——— H———, and of course I am that man . . . and I thank you and have found it a privilege and an honor to have met you.

Yours truly,
C——— H———

New life through a new self-image? Yes, it can be done—through personal application of the techniques of creative psycho-cybernetics.

You can do it, too.

GUIDELINES

1. Look at yourself in the mirror, but look behind your face to your inner self.

2. This self-image does not rule you; you rule it. Drawing up your mental blueprint, you shape your destiny in terms of your plans and your dreams. You are a statesman, a Founding Father, and you give yourself a Bill of Rights.

3. Build your self-image from past successes, and you will create a happy, successful individual.

4. If you try to build on past failures, you will distort the mental picture and lay the groundwork for frustration and misery.

5. You cannot think positively with negative beliefs; by the same token, you cannot think negatively with constructive beliefs.

6. Forget your age. You can change your concept of yourself at any age. Escape from the tomb of yesterday and erect a proud monument to tomorrow.

7. Your image of yourself must have some foundation in reality. You must believe your picture of yourself will fit into your scheme of things.

8. The first step in creating a new self-image is to rise above negation and to convince yourself of the pos-

sibility of a richer, fuller life through your self-image power.

Principles to Live By

1. Your self-image must be yours alone—not someone else's, not culture-bound, not enslaved to consensus.

2. Incorporate; offer the outer you and the inner you full partnership.

3. Every day tell yourself that you were born into the world to succeed, not to fail.

4. When the breaks are going against you, try all the harder, and stand strongly behind the one thing you can really count on: your faith in yourself.

5. A goal for all days and all seasons: develop your self-image.

6. See your big self daily and you will lose your fear of competition.

7. Selflessness is a false notion. Refuse to allow such fantasy to lure you away from the sustaining force in your life: confidence in yourself.

8. Every day work to create a pleasant climate inside yourself, with sunshine warming you from within and no gale warnings.

9. Daily, reactivate your success mechanism. Stoke it with confidence and enthusiasm and inspiring goals. No fuel shortage within you, and no rationing.

EXERCISE

You are seated in a cozy room in the playhouse of your mind, relaxing, daydreaming, eyes closed, meditating in a green oasis.

In big block letters is the word IMAGE; you envision this displayed word and you see yourself writing it on paper with pencil or pen or on a mirror with lipstick.

You have a message for yourself, and it is more important to you than any of the headline news on television. "I will not be ten inches small with frustration," you tell yourself, "when I can reach the height of ten feet with the use of confidence from past successes. Today— and tomorrow—and every day I will blot irrelevance from my mind and concentrate on fundamentals, I will reach out toward the positive, the successful, side of myself. I will struggle to keep the faith—in myself."

Thoughts to Live By

1. *Things will change for the better when you do.* Renounce passivity. Take an active, ongoing approach to life.

2. *A healthy self-image is your best friend.* But, just as you must give to a friendship to sustain its growth, you must give wholeheartedly to your constant companion, your self-image. If you do, your image will support you in any crisis—and you will never feel alone or inadequate.

Chapter 2

The New Successful You:
A Professional Human Being

This is an age of specialization. As men and machines grope toward solutions to the complexities of a technological society, their skills become increasingly precise. People are engaged in professions today that are more and more demanding in terms of human control and personal effort.

Vocationally, professional skills are essential to the growth of our modern culture. But work skills alone will not bring people to happiness. More is required: qualities inhering in each individual, concepts, imaging patterns, attitudes. What it comes down to is this: You must be more than a vocational professional to qualify for citizenship in the great land of inner peace and tranquillity; you must make yourself a professional human being.

In this book, you can share a thrilling adventure in the theater of your mind, in the playhouse of your mind. Tune inward now, and watch this drama unfold.

CASE HISTORY

DOCTOR: How old are you, Mr. Williams?

WILLIAMS: Twenty-seven.

DOCTOR: How tall?

WILLIAMS: Six feet three.

DOCTOR: And what is your problem? Tell me what motivated you to consult me.

WILLIAMS: I have a ghastly inferiority complex.

DOCTOR: What do you mean by that?

WILLIAMS: Fear stalks me morning, noon, and night.

DOCTOR: What do you fear?

WILLIAMS: Failing as a human being. Even here with you, Doctor, in your office, I feel uncomfortable.

DOCTOR: Why?

WILLIAMS: I don't know, but I am constantly on guard. I watch out to avoid stepping on the toes of other people.

DOCTOR: Are you married?

WILLIAMS: Yes, I have two children—a girl five years old and a boy of three.

DOCTOR: And your mate?

WILLIAMS: She is a housewife.

DOCTOR: Your occupation?

WILLIAMS: Student at a computer program school—computer operations in various languages.

DOCTOR: Do you communicate through your personal computer?

WILLIAMS: I don't know. Probably not. Communication with myself is difficult. I guess I never appreciate myself.

DOCTOR: Tell me about the rest of your family.

WILLIAMS: I have two sisters. One works for the Welfare Department and the other stays home with my mother.

DOCTOR: What about your father?

WILLIAMS: I haven't seen him for many years. One day he just walked out of the house. He didn't come back.

DOCTOR: You're six feet three?

WILLIAMS: Yes.

DOCTOR: When you look in the mirror, what do you see?

WILLIAMS: Myself.

DOCTOR: Of course, but what kind of self?

WILLIAMS: The outward portion. The inner me tries to dictate to the outer me.

DOCTOR: And what is the internal man telling you?

WILLIAMS: Not to be fearful.

DOCTOR: Tell me, how big is this man inside you?

WILLIAMS: About this big *(separating thumb and index finger)*. Three inches.

DOCTOR: Why only three inches?

WILLIAMS: Perhaps because I came from a broken home.

DOCTOR: Are you sensitive?

WILLIAMS: Yes, bashful. Since the age of sixteen. Eleven years later, I am the same.

DOCTOR: And you feel responsible for your broken home?

WILLIAMS: No, but there is a barrier inside me.

DOCTOR: What about your relations with your wife?

WILLIAMS: My emotional difficulties stagger me. Raising children, I am not equipped to give them what they need.

DOCTOR: Do you give your wife what she needs?

WILLIAMS: I give her trouble.

DOCTOR: In what way?

WILLIAMS: I lose myself in this dungeon in my mind. I disappear, and find relief with another woman.

DOCTOR: Does this *really* give you relief?

WILLIAMS: No.

DOCTOR: What is your present income?

WILLIAMS: I'm living on Welfare. Had no formal education, just graduated from high school. After enrolling in the computer program, I figured I'd go on to college. But my life is not a continuous rhythm—just up and down. Sometimes, by myself, I get so depressed I cry. I'm six feet three and I cry like a baby.

DOCTOR: Why do you cry?

WILLIAMS: I am obsessed with being fired, even when I have a job to support my family.

DOCTOR: Were you in the war?

WILLIAMS: Yes, G.I. Bill, student loan to participate in the computer program—up to my neck in debts.

DOCTOR: What bothers you most?

WILLIAMS: That I am unable to appreciate the gift of life and make progress each day. I wish to identify with the universe.

33

DOCTOR: That's fine. Still, do you know what you must do first before you can achieve such an identity?

WILLIAMS: Appreciate that I'm alive.

DOCTOR: And what will make you feel this?

WILLIAMS: Losing my fears.

DOCTOR: What one basic thing do you lack?

WILLIAMS: The possession of being.

DOCTOR: I'll buy that. Can you tell me the meaning of "possession of being"?

WILLIAMS: Knowing myself fully.

DOCTOR: What is the essential ingredient in knowing yourself?

WILLIAMS: Being happy with myself.

DOCTOR: And what is the basic ingredient in happiness?

WILLIAMS: Being truthful with myself.

DOCTOR: Do you hate yourself?

WILLIAMS: Yes and no.

DOCTOR: Do you possess courage?

WILLIAMS: I believe so.

DOCTOR: Do you accept yourself?

WILLIAMS: When I do something right.

DOCTOR: What about compassion for yourself?

WILLIAMS: No, I don't have compassion for myself.

DOCTOR: Why not?

WILLIAMS: I don't accomplish enough. I never climb out of the rut.

DOCTOR: Nobody is perfect and, indeed, perfectionism is a grave liability. You must learn to accept yourself as you are.

WILLIAMS: I never had a father image on which to pattern my behavior.

DOCTOR: I understand, but you are different from your father. Even your fingerprints are different. You can't hold yourself responsible for his lacks.

WILLIAMS: I know this, but I can't shrug off this feeling.

DOCTOR: Yes you can. With self-respect. Have you any?

WILLIAMS: No.

DOCTOR: Baby, that's your problem.

WILLIAMS: My only problem?

DOCTOR: No. We all have hang-ups. But your lack of self-respect—isn't this your worst hang-up? That's why—though six feet three—a little self dominates your mirror. Three inches small. I'm tired of hearing about dungeons of resentment. I want to hear of self-respect. You must learn to accept yourself with all your imperfections. When you respect yourself, you can't hate yourself or anyone else—not even your father. Forgive yourself—forgive your father.

WILLIAMS: I can't.

DOCTOR: You must. If only to give your children the self-respect your father could not give you. Is this asking too much?

WILLIAMS: I guess not. That's why I came to see you.

DOCTOR: You don't need my help—you need to help yourself.

WILLIAMS: How?

DOCTOR: Can you learn to handle computers?

WILLIAMS: Yes.

DOCTOR: Then you can learn to become expert with the computer in your midbrain, your Creative Mechanism, your success mechanism, the tape recorder of your experiences. Think in negative terms and, calling upon past failures, you will fail before you start.

Use the confidence of past successes in your present undertaking and you will succeed. You cannot think positively with negative feelings any more than you can think negatively with positive feelings. I place my pen on the table. Now, effortlessly, I pick it up. As an infant, when I tried to do this I zigzagged and could not master this simple task. Yet, finally learning how, what happened to the zigzag habit? I forgot it and remembered only the successful performance—for the remainder of my life. In the same fashion, you can pick up success and happiness, if you will remember your greatest treasure—your self-respect as a professional human being. Got the message?

[NARRATOR: A year later Williams visits the doctor.]

DOCTOR: Any hang-ups about your father?

WILLIAMS: No. I forgave him and myself too. I have a job as a computer specialist. I make my wife happy—sometimes anyway. And I am finally a good father to my lovely children.

HOMEWORK

And now another pencil-and-paper exercise to help you earn an A where it counts—with yourself. Work carefully on this assignment, just as if three credits were involved. In truth, you can afford to fail a few courses so long as you ultimately become a professional human being. You won't fail in the long run, however, because you will have the basic capacity to channel your energies into constructive paths.

Twin questions here: What ten things do I admire in myself? What ten qualities do I detest in myself?

The purpose of this assignment is to launch an initial effort to discover the nature of your self-image and thereby move toward becoming a professional human being. Persons unfamiliar with such self-analysis may have trouble finding ten likes and dislikes.

Typical "likes":

Comfortable feeling with people; ability to admit faults; increasing mental competence; capacity to derive pleasure from creative people, books, and lectures; growing self-discipline in key areas; freedom to become oneself; acceptance of God, ability to love self and others; expanding ego strength; strong native intelligence; spontaneous, attractive, dependable; capacity for self-criticism; tolerance of others' constructive criticism, and desire for growth; enjoyment of little things; cheerfulness and self-confidence; feelings of worthiness; responsible attitudes; honesty and integrity.

Typical "dislikes":

Dishonest critical attitude toward others; playing God; misdirected aggressiveness; lack of empathy; insecurity and hopelessness; overconcerned with others' reactions; overemotional and overreacting, insensitive to people; distrustful attitudes; too easily offended; spiteful and vindictive; self-conscious and moody; inadequacy in coping with problems; egotistical and self-centered; inability to relax; shaky personal ethics and values; opinionated and dogmatic; lacking in spontaneity; talking too much without listening; guilt-ridden and self-pitying.

QUESTIONS AND ANSWERS

Q. What helps plants and animals to live and to reproduce their species?

A. A built-in guidance system.

Q. Why is man's guidance system more versatile than those of the lower animals?

A. Only man has emotional and spiritual needs. He lives in three worlds: the mind, the spirit, the body.

Q. Why is man's built-in guidance system a creative success mechanism?

A. It was designed to guide man to successful living. Man's free will, however, can distort the mechanism, steering it to failure rather than to success.

Q. If our self-like exceeds our self-dislike, is the success mechanism working efficiently?

A. Not necessarily. With too much self-like, we may blind ourselves to obvious defects. Conversely, when there is a preponderance of self-dislike, we may deal too harshly with ourselves.

Q. What is the significant difference between the guidance systems of plants and animals and the mechanism in man?

A. Man possesses free will. We can set and change goals, exercising creative imagination.

Q. Can you define creative imagination?

A. Except when used negatively, all imagination is creative.

Q. In what two ways do we utilize the success mechanism?

A. First, to steer us toward goals or to adjust ourselves to the environment. Second, to solve problems.

Q. How do we make use of "negative feedback" with the success mechanism?

A. "Negative feedback" warns us that if we are not living properly we must change. As with missiles and other mechanical homing devices, this principle is utilized to adjust our course.

Q. How can the mechanism respond successfully after previous failures?

A. It recalls the successes, forgets the failures, and repeats the successful behavior without additional conscious thought.

Q. Can the success mechanism use imagination or reasoning power?

A. No, it is a faithful reactor. It operates on self-concepts and goals supplied by the forebrain.

Q. Does the success mechanism set goals and determine whether they remain valid?

A. No. Original and revised goals must be formulated by the forebrain. If the forebrain does not furnish new goals, the mechanism will function indefinitely in a routine pattern.

Q. What about the success mechanism in problem solving or in probing for fresh ideas?

A. It acts as a scanner, reviewing stored knowledge and memories.

Q. And is there an answer inside us already?

A. Apparently, there is an infinite storehouse of ideas,

knowledge, and power to which the success mechanism has access.

Q. Does one determine to change the self-image on the spur of the moment?

A. No. One must have a strong basis for deciding the old self-image is faulty. You must feel the new self-concept is both true and consistent with your real self.

Q. How do we know we are "engineered for success"?

A. Man came into this world to succeed, not to fail. This has been proved. We were created by a power greater than ourselves which wishes none of us to fail.

Q. What incentive will prod our success mechanism to operate efficiently?

A. A sharply defined goal or target. A vague objective will not suffice. It must be a real goal, not a matter of wishful thinking.

Q. How must we look upon our objective?

A. As though it already existed.

Q. Why plan in terms of end results?

A. Our success mechanism supplies the means for establishing clear-cut goals.

Q. Should we fear mistakes?

A. Not if we can profit from negative feedback and adjust our conduct more successfully.

Q. How does one learn skills?

A. Trial and error is the name of the game. Continue to correct until successful, forgetting past errors, recalling and utilizing the successful response. This faculty is a prerequisite for becoming a professional human being.

Your Great Automatic Mechanism

What is your most important tool in establishing yourself as a bona fide professional human being? Your inbuilt automatic mechanism.

This is an impersonal mechanism in the sense that, like all servomechanisms, it relies upon memory and it works upon the data which we funnel into it. If, through our thinking and imaging processes, we feed it positive data, it will process the data with this orientation; if, on the other hand, we give it data that is negative, it will function with negative results. Thus it acts as a success mechanism or as a failure mechanism.

Obviously, you must learn to use it as a success mechanism. If you master this art, without attending medical school or law school or worrying about credits or licensing procedures, you become a professional. The highest caliber professional, in this age of depersonalization, overconformity, and cynicism, is a professional human being.

First, you must understand that your great automatic mechanism operates in terms of objectives. Give it a specific goal, and this guidance system will steer you toward it. But this goal must be visualized so sharply that your brain and nervous system accept it as real.

Remember this: Your great mechanism cannot differentiate between an imagined experience and a real one. What you picture as true becomes data fed into the mechanism and is acted upon. Thus, if you image failure vividly, it assumes a reality to your nervous system, which will give out failure-type responses. Similarly, if you see yourself as successful, you are on your way to success.

A number of years ago *Research Quarterly* related an experiment that illustrates this point splendidly. In a twenty-day test, two groups of students worked to increase their effectiveness as basketball sharpshooters. One group practiced shooting at the basket every day; their marksmanship improved 24 percent by the twentieth day. The other group devoted twenty minutes a day to *imagining* they were throwing the ball into the basket. Incredibly, their accuracy soared 23 percent.

This experiment underlines the supreme importance of making your great Creative Mechanism a success mechanism, and leads us into an analysis of how you go about lubricating this mechanism.

1. *Formulate worthwhile goals to feed into your guidance system.* This process of goal setting is very important, and it is also important that you do not confine yourself to lifetime objectives but set daily goals, too, so that each day can stand on its own as a vital entity, as a time span in which you can achieve objectives for which you feel enthusiasm.

2. *Concentrate on these end results.* Of course, the means are significant also, but you must understand that the in-built automatic mechanism will supply the means when you specify the goal.

3. *Lose your dread of temporary failure.* Everybody makes mistakes and suffers setbacks. If your fear of failure inhibits your setting of goals, you fail before you start.

4. *Rely on trial and error.* This is how you learn skills and establish successes. Eventually, you learn to forget your mistakes and you assimilate your successful patterns into habits that will guide you toward added success and happiness.

5. *Trust your great Creative Mechanism.* What I mean by "trust" is that you must develop a faith that if you initiate a flow of the correct type of data, this mechanism will work effectively upon it without conscious effort on your part. If you try to force it, you will jam up the mechanism and it will not function properly.

Living Psycho-Cybernetics

My theory of creative psycho-cybernetics has helped millions of people to live more satisfying lives. It is no mere abstraction, no ivory tower concept. It is a theory that works for people today in this world.

Still, to doubt is natural, and surely the proof is in the pudding, so let me quote two letters. The first is from a civic-minded chartered life underwriter for a large insurance company.

Dear Dr. Maltz:

During the last five years, we in our local Boy Scout Council have made repeated attempts to have greater penetration into the inner-city areas. Where we have one-third of all boys between the ages of eight and fourteen participating in the Boy Scout movement in other parts of the Council, we have less than ten percent enjoying the benefits in this "last chance" area. However, not only here but in all areas of boy development we see negative thoughts, poor self-image, and lack of self-reliance invading the youth of our world today.

Until about ten years ago, I too lived in this poor self-image vacuum with a negative attitude. Then you and your books became a part of my life. I heard you speak at the Life Underwriters Meeting at the University of Redlands; and this year my wife is taking a course under the auspices of Cerritos College with your book *Psycho-Cybernetics* as a textbook. It is exciting to see your book in every bookstore and on every book counter. During the past year, I have been thinking of you in connection with the great Boy Scout movement. I have been speculating on the prospect of your goal-setting, self-image psychology being implemented in the young people beginning at age eight. Why must they wait until they are adult, as I did when I first heard about you? Why couldn't we plant the seed in young boys' minds beginning at age eight and expanding through age eighteen— "he is as he thinks he is all day long." This last weekend, October 19 and 20, at the Regional Convention of BSA, it became a must that I write you as you are the key to unlocking the door of these young people's minds. I feel so strongly that the problem of the black and the brown are due to a poor self-image.

Dr. Maltz, I can visualize parts of every advancement in Scouting devoted to your teaching. I can visualize one-third of the boys in the United States receiving a message from you as they progress up the Boy Scout trail. I can visualize the message printed in many languages throughout this worldwide youth movement. I can visualize the skill of boys discovering their success mechanism within them through the Boy Scout Handbook, a publication second only to the Bible in numbers.

Today, I am fifty-three, Camping Chairman and President-Elect of the Long Beach Area California Council of Boy Scouts of America with 10,000 boys, and the proud holder of the Silver Beaver Award. These great things have happened to me because of you. It is my sincere hope that the same thing will happen to millions of boys throughout the world also, because of you. I am looking forward to hearing of your ideas.

Sincerely,
Lewis N. Hindley, Jr.

The second letter was forwarded to me from *Reader's Digest*.

Dear Dr. Maltz:

Fan mail on your book continues to come in, as witness this letter, quoted below:

"As a reader of the *Digest* for over thirty years, I wish to congratulate you most highly for publishing a condensation of Dr. Maltz's wonderfully good 'Book Section'— 'Your Built-in Success Mechanism,' in the April 1961 edition of your *Digest*.

"As an indication of my opinion of its value and quality, after I had studied the book itself, *Psycho-Cybernetics,* for over a month, I ordered another copy to send to my daughter as a present. In my forwarding letter to her, I wrote: 'After a careful study of this book, it is my honest opinion that it is the most valuable one published in the past 1500 years.'

S. A. Loftus"

Well, 1500 years is a good long span of time. I'd say this tribute was pretty hard to top.

Sincerely,
Maurice T. Ragsdale
Book Editor

GUIDELINES

1. An electronic computer about the size of a hazelnut is in our midbrain, tape-recording our experiences.

2. In the forebrain is the seat of our goals activating a sense of fulfillment.

3. When we wish to reach a goal, we call upon our tape recorder to organize this effort. If we feed in failure experiences, we will fail; if we nourish it with successful images and good feelings from the past, we will succeed.

4. The computer cannot rule us. We rule the computer, planting the seeds of success or failure.

5. Since we picture ourselves ten inches frustration-small and ten feet success-tall, we must strive to consolidate the positive image of ourselves.

6. Do not fear making mistakes; the business of creative living is rising above human frailty to success.

7. The professional human being develops the capacity to rise above blunders, misfortunes, and heartaches.

8. Learn to think and act in terms of solid objectives.

9. Rely on your Creative Mechanism to get the job done. Don't jam it with anxiety or forcing techniques. It will work for you subconsciously once your forebrain takes hold of a specific productive goal.

1. "Cybernetics" is derived from a Greek word meaning "helmsman," a man who steers a ship. "Psycho-cybernetics" is a word I coined to mean steering your mind to a productive goal, arriving at your destination, the greatest port in the world, peace of mind. Psycho-cybernetics is more than positive thinking; it involves positive doing.

2. I became a plastic surgeon through practice. So does every professional—every dentist, general practitioner, writer—all become expert through practice. But the most successful of all professionals is the professional human being. How do you become a professional human being? Through practice, rising above problems, leaping the hurdles of difficulties, and practicing again.

3. Every day you seek to improve yourself as a human being, hunting for the best in yourself.

4. You may be a mistake-maker but, more important, you are a mistake-breaker.

5. You forgive others and forgive yourself for today's mistakes and for all the mistakes of yesterday.

6. You incinerate the garbage of negative feelings, evicting them from your mind, searching every day to find the big you, realizing that happiness cannot exist in solitary confinement but only when you extend it with open arms to other people.

7. You rise above your little self by keeping up with *yourself*, not with the Joneses.

8. You battle to unearth in yourself a rebirth of precious feelings and images that make your life a fruitful enterprise.

9. Adjusting from destruction to construction, from cynicism to faith, from self-hatred to self-acceptance, practicing to build a more rewarding life, you enlist the success mechanism as an invaluable recruit in your crusade for creative living today.

· An Inside Job

When we speak of an inside job, we usually mean a carefully contrived crime executed by "people in the know." If a bank is robbed and there are no clues, it may be an inside job. If a home is rifled, with valuable jewelry missing, and the theft was executed with trim, neat dispatch, no complications at all, we ask ourselves if this perfect crime was not an inside job.

But the most pernicious kind of inside job is the crime we inflict upon ourselves when, through fear or hatred, we rob ourselves of our sense of worth. Another form of self-robbery is procrastination—letting our goals wait until tomorrow. We rob ourselves of peace of mind when we persist in endless self-criticism. Indeed, we create prison walls around us, preventing our achievement of happiness. Are you an "inside jobber" who walks away from reality into the gloomy tunnels of a disturbed mind? Do you hurl yourself into a dungeon of futility?

If you do, do not despair, because psycho-cybernetics is an inside job—a creative inside job. You can change. This kind of inside job will improve your self-image and will help you to grow in stature as a professional human being. This creative inside job will bolster your belief in yourself as you rise above your mistakes to self-respect and compassion. You refuse to make a mountain from a molehill, performing daily tasks without pressure. What is your inside job? To use your Creative Mechanism for success, not for failure, to achieve stature as a professional human being.

EXERCISE

Again, you seat yourself comfortably in the lovely green playhouse of your mind, a garden of Eden. The greenery brings peace to your heart.

You prepare to fortify yourself for a new role in life, as a winner.

Pencil and paper in hand, you print the word EVOLUTION—or you could block it on your bathroom mirror with lipstick or crayon (if your household is indulgent).

You are once again straining to break through to the successful side of yourself. "This is my evolution," you tell yourself. "Not in a Darwinian sense, not with cosmic overtones, but my evolution from failure to success. I will seize the glorious opportunity to use my gift of life, I will embark upon a pilgrimage to a wonderful land where I shall reside as a professional human being. Unquenchably, I shall offer friendship to myself, and this friendship will not falter in crises. I have stumbled and I have walked the earth in blindness, but now I have found my vocation as a professional human being. My goal? To be a brother to myself and to others."

Thoughts to Live By

1. *Demand results from yourself*. Challenge is not merely tension; it is also satisfaction.

2. *Negative feelings are thieves of time*. Even if you are powerless to make our streets safe, you are not powerless to arrest and banish the robbers of your peace of mind.

Chapter 3

Imagination: The Playhouse of Your Mind

Imagination is what you make it. It is a precious gift. Do you use it wisely or squander it?

The imagination is a curious mixture of complexities and contradictions, and it overflows with possibilities.

Last year, I attended a reunion of my old college classmates. There they were, these doughty survivors of the grim hazards of time, most of them gray-haired or white-haired, foreheads wrinkled, their physical youth escaped. I exchanged handshakes and greetings with some of these old acquaintances and one fellow said to me, "Max, you have aged," and he seemed surprised.

Believe me, he didn't hurt my feelings, for I do admit to being somewhat over twenty-one, but his comment indicated to me that in *his* imagination *he* was still young.

Yes, the imagination is a marvelous wonderland, funny and sad, but this chapter is on the *playhouse* of your mind, so let's get on with the play.

CASE HISTORY

[NARRATOR: Pierre is a fine-looking man. He sits opposite the doctor in the consultation room. At forty-five he has a full crop of black hair, graying near the temples. But his eyes are sad.]

DOCTOR: What is your problem?

PIERRE: I feel tense, hypertense. Hunger pains assail me in

the middle of the night and I feel I have to raid the refrigerator.

DOCTOR: Anything else?

PIERRE: I don't sleep well. I toss and turn and wake up, terrified, from nightmares.

DOCTOR: Do you understand why?

PIERRE: No, but perhaps they result from fatigue.

DOCTOR: Can you describe the nature of your tension?

PIERRE: Well, I'm a worrier from way back, always negative, looking at the gloomy side of things.

DOCTOR: Why?

PIERRE: Family influence maybe. My father would say "Don't do this!" and my mother would say "Don't do that!" When I was a boy, I began to doubt my competence.

DOCTOR: What do you do for a living?

PIERRE: I teach piano and compose.

DOCTOR: From what do you believe you feel tension?

PIERRE: The conflict between the piano and the composition.

DOCTOR: Is this really a conflict?

PIERRE: To me it is.

DOCTOR: I think it's a happy conflict. Few people create these days. Aren't you blessed?

PIERRE: I feel negative and inhibited and I always end up crawling into a shell. God knows, I've always felt shy. When I was five, I would run upstairs when people came to the house.

DOCTOR: You're still there, upstairs. You must come *downstairs* to *yourself*. Tell me, do you play the piano well? Do you compose well?

PIERRE: I think so, but I never had much of a chance.

DOCTOR: You must *create* your chances. You must *make* your opportunities by a proper use of imagination. Don't crawl around on your *knees*. You should feel gratified that you are able to compose music and play the piano. Are you inhibited because the world has not accepted you as a composer?

49

PIERRE: Yes. I feel a very deep sense of failure.

DOCTOR: Do you want to continue composing and playing the piano?

PIERRE: Yes.

DOCTOR: Then you must get rid of negative feelings and accept yourself as a person who came into this world to succeed. *Forget* yesterday and *live today. Now!* You're no longer a boy of five running *upstairs* to hide when people are *downstairs.*

PIERRE: Upstairs is safer.

DOCTOR: Perhaps. But come *downstairs* and meet people—even if you get hurt. Compose creatively downstairs, live creatively downstairs, use your imagination creatively downstairs. Get your feet wet and take your chances in life. If you make a mistake, that doesn't mean you are a failure for life. Don't you erase the wrong notes when you compose? Then erase your social errors. Give yourself another chance. This is what *life* is about. Tell me, where are you now?

PIERRE: Sometimes upstairs, sometimes downstairs.

DOCTOR: Stay *downstairs!*

PIERRE: I lack courage; I'm afraid.

DOCTOR: Courage comes from *trying,* even if you get hurt. Camus, the French philosopher, said: "Greatness consists in *trying* to be great." It's the same with courage. You build your own courage. Here's an exercise; do it. Take your wife's lipstick and write the word *me* on the mirror. Leave it there all week and, every day, when you shave, say to yourself: "I'm two me's. Ten inches small upstairs when I live in the past and ten feet tall downstairs when I live in the present." Play a new composition *downstairs*—not the old one *upstairs.* Use your imagination creatively.

[NARRATOR: Pierre's wife, who plays and teaches the organ, has been listening. She wipes her eyes with a handkerchief and says:]

WIFE: Why don't you write a new composition, Pierre, and call it "Downstairs"?

PIERRE: Good idea.

DOCTOR: Bravo!

[NARRATOR: A week later Pierre and his wife return to consult the doctor.]

DOCTOR: Well?

PIERRE: I came down two steps, but I didn't plunge.

DOCTOR: It's a good start. You tried and you'll get there.

PIERRE: I wrote a composition called "Two Steps Down." (*He goes to the piano and plays the short piece. It is very humorous, with staccato notes of hesitation and doubt and suddenly, at the end, two determined steps.*)

DOCTOR: Terrific.

PIERRE: But I'm still afraid, Doctor.

DOCTOR: Your fear is not *exclusive*. Every human being feels afraid sometimes, but resourceful people turn crises into creative opportunities.

PIERRE: The trouble is, my goals are beyond my reach.

DOCTOR: You're not Beethoven or Chopin. Be yourself; set goals within your capabilities.

PIERRE: But what about my hang-up, the clash between composing and making a living?

DOCTOR: You and your wife both teach. You make a living, and you also make a living for that man *inside of you* when you compose. Do one composition at a time— *downstairs.*

[NARRATOR: Three months later a smile lighted up Pierre's face. He handed the doctor a musical composition called "Downstairs." Pierre had begun to find his true self, in the present. Free of inhibition, no longer concerned with the mistakes of yesterday, he had learned to use his imagination productively.]

Again, a classroom assignment with pad and pencil; or perhaps you would like to chalk it up on the blackboard of your mind (but do not erase).

Your task is to imagine personal success, to solidify the positive mental image in your consciousness, and thus to pave the way for future imaginative successes to help the growth of your healthy self-image.

Examples:

Discussing sex adequately with an adolescent son.

Delivering a speech to the local chapter of an organization.

Asking the boss for a raise, and getting it.

Standing up to a bully.

Escaping tactfully from a long-winded, boring conversation.

Handling a fractious teen-ager.

Conquering stage fright or your fear of darkness or heights.

Selling an original idea.

Improving your gamesmanship.

QUESTIONS AND ANSWERS

Q. Why is it we act, feel, or perform as we do?

A. Because of what we *imagine* is the truth about ourselves and our environment.

Q. Is willpower related to this?

A. Somewhat, but the power flows mainly from imagination. As an illustration, picture yourself walking a 12-inch plank on the living-room floor. No problem, right? Now, visualize a pair of 20-story buildings separated by a narrow alley. Place the plank across the alley, and proceed to walk across it. Now, what happens to willpower?

Q. How does the nervous system differentiate between our imagined and our real experiences?

A. It doesn't. It reacts to our concept of what is true, regardless of whether it is rational.

Q. How does hypnotizing a subject illustrate that imagination is more potent than will?

A. Under hypnosis, the subject believes whatever the hypnotist says and (within some limits) obeys commands unquestioningly.

Q. Do we react to what is really around us or to what we imagine is reality?

A. Rightly or wrongly, we respond to what we believe is true.

Q. How can we utilize our imagination in the pursuit of success?

A. Vividly imagine successful achievement of cherished goals.

Q. When can imagination spell failure?

A. If the concepts and mental images are distorted, the reaction to environment will be inappropriate.

Q. What are some illustrations of the use of imagination for success?

A. Chess: Alekhine defeating Capablanca by training for three months, playing chess solely in his mind.

Sales: Picturing difficult sales situations and playing the role of handling them successfully.

Employment: Rehearsing the potential details of the interview in advance; anticipating a wide range of possible questions and planning appropriate answers.

Piano playing: Imagining the keyboard and practicing in the head. An authority recommends memorizing and reviewing a new composition before playing it on the piano.

Golf: Visualizing the perfect shot, the "feel" of the club, the trajectory of the ball.

Soldiering: Napoleon's utilization of imagination to practice battles in advance of the engagement.

Business: Conrad Hilton imagining he was in the hotel business long before purchasing a hotel. Henry Kaiser picturing each business venture before it was a reality.

Q. What do these forms of using the imagination to improve the self-image illustrate?

A. The power of positive thinking and positive doing.

Q. The power of positive thinking does not always work. Why was it effective in these illustrations?

A. Because it was consistent with the self-image. When it is inconsistent, no amount of courage or willpower will enable the individual to succeed.

Q. Picturing the desired objective combines what two factors?

A. A sharply focused mental image of the end result, and true belief in its attainment; both are necessary.

Q. How do we find the best part of ourselves?

A. We must evaluate our present goals, visualize those we wish to change—and we must use our imagination to "see" ourselves in our new roles.

Q. Can mental patients improve themselves by imagining they are normal?

A. It is interesting that patients who imagined themselves well adjusted improved their early test scores substantially.

Q. How can we fathom the truth about the potential of our real self-image?

A. Use the success mechanism as a scanner and problem solver. Meditate, then act. Psycho-cybernetics means steering your mind to a productive useful goal within your training and capabilities.

Q. What is a valid test of the caliber of self-image?

A. How we live our daily lives. What we profess does not equal the impact of actual conduct.

Q. How does enriched living begin?

A. With vivid, oft-repeated pictures of constructive goals.

Q. How was our present self-image formed?

A. By interpretations of environment and experiences.

Q. How can we rely on this technique to build a healthier self-image?

A. Establish realistic goals; devote a half hour each day to vivid, detailed imagery surrounding them, not only seeing the goals but visualizing their achievement.

Q. How should we see ourselves acting?

A. Appropriately, successfully, realistically.

Q. Need we worry about whether this goal will "work"?

A. The nervous system will take care of it automatically if we practice with discipline.

Q. When, during a relaxed period of about a half hour, we say, "I will act this way tomorrow," what are we saying?

A. We are relying on willpower.

Q. Is there a better way?

A. Imagining yourself acting this way—now, for half an hour, today.

Q. What additional attitudes are helpful?

A. Imagine feeling already the desired personality. We see ourselves free of timidity, moving confidently among people, poised and assured. We see ourselves behaving calmly in situations that formerly panicked us. The new attitude makes us feel expansive.

Q. What difference is there between this approach and an exercise of willpower?

A. Without willpower, we respond spontaneously, without constructive rehearsal.

Q. Why do we receive this type of response from our success mechanism?

A. The mechanism operates on experiences, whether real or fancied, and when we program into it powerful imaginary experiences it functions as if they were true.

The Fabulous Power of Imagination

Now, let us summarize in thumbnail form the message of this chapter. Your imagination is a powerhouse. Potentially, it can jet-propel you to success or bury you in a quicksand of failure.

Your goal in finding new meaning in life is to strengthen your self-image through a reactivation of your automatic servomechanism, making it a success mechanism rather than a failure mechanism.

How do you do this?

Through a positive use of your imagination.

There are two sides to the coin. I know this because I have seen both sides.

As a second-year medical student in my early twenties, my imagination was a storehouse of negative thoughts that led me to worry and agitation. Oral quizzes terrified me. I would anticipate them with dread and my agitation drove me from shyness to ineptitude to despondency. I knew my subject, but when called upon to answer in front of the other students, I forgot everything I knew in my nervousness. In a course in pathology, I became so unsettled that I feared the professor would fail me and that the goal of my life would escape my grasp.

Written examinations were no problem. I was calm and knowledgeable. Peering through a microscope at a slide, I would analyze it with professional competence.

But my troubles with negative imagination threatened to undo my grasp of the subject matter. At the thought of an oral quiz, I would break out in a cold sweat and images of disaster would overwhelm my mind.

Then, suddenly, a fresh thought came to me. "Suppose, when the professor asks me a question, I stand up and answer while pretending that I am writing it on a sheet of paper without seeing the face of anyone in the classroom." Could this help me?

Yes, this positive use of imagination helped me. And, believe me, it has helped millions of other people.

Imagination, destructive and negative, or imagination, constructive and positive. They are as different as night and day, darkness and sunshine, failure and success.

It is in our imagination that we produce the data that is fed into our automatic servomechanism and leads us upward to achievement or downward to defeat.

Imagination is not mathematical, so you can't measure it in any specific sense. You can't eat it or count it or smoke it or touch it or smell it or see it or drink it. But it is there inside you, a staggeringly powerful force which you must learn to master.

So powerful is the imagination that great actors use it to transform their personalities. On stage, using their imagination, they *are* somebody else. Not just an internal feeling, for they *convey* another person so unmistakably that audiences are willing to suspend disbelief and accept their portrayals.

Using your imagination you navigate. In your mind, your boat sails through the rough seas of frustration, rolling toward fresh horizons, unseen destinations, and, most basic, toward creation of a new, shining self-image.

Voyaging through the crucial inner space of your mind, you discover that the world within you is not flat with despair. Like Christopher Columbus, you learn that the world is round—and, indeed, inside your mind it is round so that your hands grasping for the good things in life can encircle and clasp them firmly.

Probing into the vast storehouse of imagination, you learn to enrich your life by overthrowing the habit of destructive imaging and substituting an orientation of optimism and enthusiastic goal-striving.

In a hustle-bustle world of crowded highways and frantic pedestrians, technological power and spectatoritis, polluted air and cynical morality, disillusionment and rheumatism of the spirit, you must turn for help to your imagination.

Take stock of yourself, your assets and your liabilities. Concentrate on developing your capacities and strive to reactivate your success mechanism.

View the past with perspective, and learn to look realistically at past mistakes, not so that you can bury yourself in shame, but so you can avoid the same mistakes in the future, and rise above them to new success patterns.

In your imagination, finally, plan for the present. Do not aim at keeping up with the Joneses or outcompeting the Smiths. Your prime motive is to compete with yourself, to exceed your past track record, to move toward new inspiring goals, improving the quality of your life, enriching your loved ones in a spiritual sense, strengthening the fibers of your confidence in yourself.

The following ideas will help you:

1. Each day we must concentrate on reaffirming the positive tone of our imagination.

2. Reality is an extension of the groundwork laid in the inner space of the mind.

3. With negative imagination, we will move toward failure; with positive imagination, we will move toward success.

4. Obsessing ourselves with past failures preconditions us for a lifetime of failures.

5. On the other hand. we turn a crisis into an opportunity when we call upon the rosy glow of past successes to help us master it and move forward.

6. Understanding that happiness and misery stem from constructive and destructive use of imagination, we focus on this powerhouse and work to control our fate.

7. In the playhouse of our mind, we write a fresh

new scenario. It is a happy story, a success story, and the hero—why, it is you.

Recently, a letter with a poem arrived in the mail. It is extremely well attuned to this subject matter, so I quote it in full:

Try, try
Forget the asking why.
Do it for the doing
But forget the means whereby.
Keep thinking of the end
And let the sleeping doggies lie.
Try, try, try.

If Psycho-Cybernetics is the way to reach a goal,
Then let me learn to use the great machine that guides my
        soul.
Let me understand the inner workings of my brain.
If I could see the world just as it is, I'm not insane.
The answers all are there but conscious reason works so slow.
The art of life is wrought by skill, not thought, I think,
        and so . . .

I'll try, try
I know I feel the why,
So I'll do it for the doing
And I'll find the means whereby.
Tomorrow is where my imagination is today
Just as much as now I'm where I dreamed of yesterday.

Sincerely yours,
Robert S. Ryan

GUIDELINES

1. The human mind is unable to differentiate between a real experience and an experience vividly imagined.

2. Every day of our lives, we use imagination positively or negatively; and this leads us to lives of frustration or achievement.

3. Reality is a product of imagination.

4. Negative imagination produces negative habits and failure results. Positive imagination produces positive habits and success results.

5. By invoking images of past successes to bolster us in our challenges of today, we can turn crises into opportunities.

6. Child abuse is a recognized crime. Abuse of the imagination is also a crime; do not commit it against yourself.

7. With constructive imagination, you enact a success story in the playhouse of your mind. This will give you added confidence in the rougher struggle to execute this scenario in the world outside.

Principles to Live By

1. Creative imagination is the launching pad of achievement.

2. Believe in yourself. Faith and belief are wings flapping en route to your destination.

3. Sincerity is a wholesome ingredient; never leave it out of the pie.

4. Refuse to enact tragedy in the playhouse of your mind. Stop playing the losing game.

5. At any age, keep your mind alive. Curious children ask questions of adults. Your childhood may be behind you, but you are never too old to maintain a healthy inquiring mind.

6. Your imagination must never surrender to despair and frustration. Your inner forces must combat the scourges of apathy and helplessness and rise above the self-defeatingness of terror.

7. Exercise your imagination psycho-cybernetically, de-

veloping the kind of data that will make your automatic mechanism a success mechanism.

EXERCISE

It is dark in the playhouse of your mind, the curtain hides the stage, and the spotlight is off. But the darkness is soothing, beneficial to your powers of concentration.

"I will try and try again," you tell yourself. "When I try to lead a better life, I use my imagination creatively. Creative imagination is the beginning of a goal; by persisting, I will reach my goal if it is within my capabilities and training. Understanding that the mind cannot differentiate between a real successful experience and one vividly imagined, I will utilize this principle to fill my mind with success images and prepare myself to win. I will imagine that I have already reached the goal and I will continue striving until I do reach it. Success in my imagination will, through sheer persistence, become real success."

Thoughts to Live By

1. *Creative imagination is a goal in the making* because you must win the battle inside before you can win it outside. The more you fortify the power of your imagination, the stronger will be your charge when you advance upon new objectives.

2. *Creative imagination is the eye of happiness.* If the eye of your imagination is blank, then the eyes of your face will lack luster. It is the inner burning glow firing your imagination which will unleash your constructive channelized aggression, and move you toward your goals. This will enable you to convert possibility into reality and to achieve happiness.

The Hope in Imagination Power

A few final words on imagination, because imagination is crucial to anything you hope to accomplish during your lifetime.

What good is your automatic mechanism if your imagination manufactures negative data?

And inspiring goals: how will they help you if, en route, your imagination conjures up terrifying visions of impending disaster?

Remember, your automatic mechanism and positive goal-setting can be basic constructive aids—but only if you are determined to win the battle over negative feelings in your imagination.

You cannot harbor a torture chamber in your imagination and live a positive life.

You cannot reel under an avalanche of nightmares and remain calm and constructive in the world.

You cannot see yourself as a Frankenstein monster and project a smile of confidence.

Therefore, you must grasp the supreme importance of the concepts and images that filter into the treasure-house of your mind. Only you can make it a treasure trove and you must feel you are worth the effort.

Keep working on the contents of your imagination. Develop a critical attitude toward negative forces that undermine you from within. Would you employ a confessed poisoner as your cook? Then use a careful screening process to keep poison out of your imagination.

Remember this: The battle begins in the inner space of your mind, and this battle you must win.

Chapter 4

Creative Dehypnosis

Are you hypnotized? Does negativism cast its dark shadow over you, obscuring the bright side of your nature with sinister gloom? This sounds morbid and theatrical? Not at all. It is a reality so unpleasant that we wish to hide from it. The truth is that millions of people bamboozle themselves with false beliefs that crush them into a sense of inferiority so severe that their pride and self-respect never see the light of day.

Do I hear dissent? You're right; but first a dramatization of my point, and later we'll resume the debate.

CASE HISTORY

DOCTOR: Your name?

WOMAN: Florence.

DOCTOR: And your problem?

FLORENCE: I want to sing.

DOCTOR: A natural instinct, certainly, but who is stopping you?

FLORENCE: Myself, I guess. At least, I never had the courage to audition.

DOCTOR: Do you sing at any specific place?

FLORENCE: I'm a soloist at church.

DOCTOR: And it is your heartfelt desire to sing elsewhere in public?

FLORENCE: Yes.

DOCTOR: Fine. But why can't you?

FLORENCE: I'm too old.

DOCTOR: You don't look old to me. How old are you?

FLORENCE: Thirty-seven.

DOCTOR: You call that old?

FLORENCE: Also, I don't know the right people.

DOCTOR: Another excuse?

FLORENCE: My technique is not fully developed.

DOCTOR: Practice makes perfect. Tell me, young lady, are you a soprano?

FLORENCE: High soprano, but always uncertain of reaching the notes from high F to high C.

DOCTOR: Do you concentrate on this task?

FLORENCE: Well, I'm not sure. I don't stick with anything. I can't seem to finish a book. I suppose I really should learn to concentrate.

DOCTOR: Yes, but everything you say is negative. If you tell yourself you won't reach the high note you won't reach it. You can't achieve with negative feelings any more than you can destroy with positive feelings. You need to believe that you can reach your goal. You must dehypnotize yourself from these negative feelings.

FLORENCE: I suppose you're right.

DOCTOR: Are you married?

FLORENCE: Yes, I have two children.

DOCTOR: Do you really want to sing, or do you make believe you want to sing? Do you wish it as a career?

FLORENCE: Yes, I think so. Yes, I do.

DOCTOR: Or do you wish to sing as a hobby?

FLORENCE: Yes.

DOCTOR: What is the difference between singing as a career and singing as a hobby?

FLORENCE: A career is my goal.

DOCTOR: Do you look at yourself with seriousness in your mirror?

FLORENCE: What do you mean?

DOCTOR: Is your appraisal honest?

FLORENCE: I see an attractive woman.

DOCTOR: Do you daydream about yesterday or do you see yourself as you are today?

FLORENCE: Today, I guess.

DOCTOR: What is your opinion of yourself?

FLORENCE: Oh, sometimes I'm a worm, but at times I am glorious.

DOCTOR: But do you like yourself?

FLORENCE: Some things about me I like.

DOCTOR: What are your good qualities?

FLORENCE: Oh, spontaneity, wit, intelligence, artistic perception. Do I sound vain and boastful? Also I enjoy good music tremendously.

DOCTOR: What do you consider to be your bad traits?

FLORENCE: Oh, I don't know. I'm sloppy and disorganized. God knows, I lose things and you could say I'm not careful about money. I don't see a thing through to the end. In a way, I'm a grasshopper jumping from one blade of grass to another.

DOCTOR: Indecisive?

FLORENCE: Impulsive and indecisive. Oh, I'm a crazy one.

DOCTOR: Psychologically do you straddle a fence?

FLORENCE: I guess so.

DOCTOR: Do you wish to jump?

FLORENCE: Jump? Yes.

DOCTOR: Where?

FLORENCE: Well, I crave fulfillment.

DOCTOR: Stop belittling yourself, friend, and dehypnotize yourself. Become a mirror watcher, and see yourself at your best. You criticize yourself too much. Kind eyes. Behold yourself with kind eyes. Sing for the fun of it. If you can't have a career, live creatively with a hobby. There are three eight-hour periods to each day: eight hours for work, eight hours for relaxation, eight hours for sleep. Practice each day during your eight hours of relaxation to perfect your singing because it gives you pleasure. Singing is your career, even if you don't make money at it. It provides you with enjoyment. Through singing, even without applause from others, you fulfill yourself and bring happiness into the world. Stop daydreaming; be realistic. Forgive yourself for your imperfections and dehypnotize yourself from self-mutilation. You can really be happy. Your indecision has led to tension, and self-denial prevents you from belting out the notes from high F to high C.

FLORENCE: I never thought of it that way.

DOCTOR: Dignity is your prime asset. If you steadfastly insist on measuring up to your dignity, you will dehypnotize yourself from negative feelings and belt out the notes from high F to high C—and your range will be magnificent.

[NARRATOR: Seven months later, Florence, all smiles, pays a return visit.]

FLORENCE: Listen to me sing, Doctor.

[NARRATOR: Standing near the piano, facing him, she launches herself into a gorgeous melody. Her tones full and rich, the room filling with her joy, she blasts off into the upper registers, soaring from high F to high C.]

DOCTOR: I applaud you, for you have dehypnotized yourself from a false belief of unworthiness. So can most of us. No matter what our calling or our situation, if we really have the desire, we can stand up to our full measure of self-respect. Let me repeat: psycho-cybernetics means steering your mind to a productive goal, and you do this *after* dehypnotizing yourself from false beliefs that keep you down.

HOMEWORK

Back to the classroom. Ask yourself this: What false faces do I wear, and what roles do I enact?

Typical false faces and roles:

Wearing a mask of contentment at social functions when at heart you feel miserable and rejected.

Nodding agreement to a person, pretending sympathetic

comprehension, when you are paying no real attention to what he is saying and caring less.

Chatting amiably with people you detest.

Prattling philosophy while plotting bedroom.

Wearing a Catholic face for Catholics, a Protestant identity for Protestants, an atheist stance for atheists, and hoping they will not compare notes.

Assuming a phony role of competence and self-assurance.

Pretending acquaintanceship with people of renown—name-dropping.

Simulating grief or joy or loyalty.

Supporting spurious arguments by referring to fictitious authorities.

"Topping" the anecdotes of others with a relentless half-concealed antagonism.

QUESTIONS AND ANSWERS

Q. How does hypnotism work?

A. It works when we believe whatever the hypnotist says, for we operate on the basis of beliefs, not upon reality or truth.

Q. What of posthypnotic suggestion?

A. In the hypnotic state, the subject is instructed to perform specific actions at a later time. If the hypnotist has blocked off memory of this instruction, the subject will perform on schedule, not knowing why he does the suggested things. Of course, he may offer absurd excuses to "prove" the rationality of his behavior.

Q. Are most of us subjected to mass hypnosis?

A. Yes. Advertisers and political organizations and many individuals attempt to persuade us with hypnotic appeals.

Q. Does this hypnosis exercise power over us?

A. Regardless of source, if we believe in the truth of

the idea, it wields the same power over us as the hypnotist's words do over his subject.

Q. Suppose someone tells you you're stupid, and you believe him?

A. You are literally hypnotized and are compelled to act stupid to be consistent with the self-conception this person has programmed into you.

Q. How widespread is mass hypnosis?

A. Most of us are to some extent hypnotized.

Q. Does hypnotism confer power on people magically? What of the stutterer, the shy, the weak?

A. Hypnotism releases self-blocking imagination. The stutterer possessed the innate capacity to speak well, the shy to have poise, the weak to feel strength—but they didn't believe in their potential. Hypnotism cleared the rubble of disbelief from the road, enabling the traffic to move forward.

Q. Where do we find the power to become happy and successful?

A. Within ourselves. But first we must dehypnotize ourselves, get rid of "I can't" attitudes.

Q. How do we become trapped by negative attitudes?

A. Other people voice doubts about us, and we adopt their negative feelings. We compare ourselves unfavorably with others. We refuse to try to change.

Q. What if we remain trapped?

A. We advertise our negative self-image and keep on blundering.

Q. How do we come to feel we are not worthy or deserving?

A. Through submitting to the brainwashing of others. If you are not worthy, who is?

Q. How would we look at a stranger with similar background who protested that he was unworthy or undeserving?

A. We might think he was displaying phony humility.

Q. How do we acquire feelings of inferiority?

A. We judge ourselves by standards of excellence. Since we are not champions at everything, we depreciate all our qualities.

Q. How should we feel about inferiority and superiority?

A. We are neither inferior nor superior; we are unique and individual.

Q. How does a person go about finding himself?

A. One must believe in his uniqueness, cultivate a deep awareness of others, and feel a sense of worth emanating from sharing his gifts with others.

Q. How did we consolidate our old beliefs about ourselves?

A. Usually without effort or strain, but with little or no exercise of willpower.

Q. What is a method for changing outworn beliefs or habits?

A. The same effortless fashion in which we acquired them.

Q. What is the function of willpower in these changes?

A. Willpower is a hindrance, reinforcing the negative habit or belief.

Q. What is better than willpower or special effort in breaking a habit?

A. Formulate a sharp mental image of the desired objective and practice toward reaching this goal.

Q. What forms of practice will help break a habit?

A. Positive practice, conscious refusal to submit. Negative practice, doing it willingly, but keeping the goal clearly in mind.

Dehypnotization and the Inferiority Complex

Let us now return to my stated thesis and resume our discussion. My point was that millions of people, nurturing false beliefs, delude themselves into feeling that they are inferior. This is, in a sense, a form of hypnosis, in that they seem unable to rebel against the depressing spell which they have cast upon themselves. They create a climate in which other people are almost forced to grant them the humiliation they feel they deserve.

In my little dramatization, Florence was this type of person, but, with assistance, she was able to dehypnotize herself and sing again. And *you* must sing again. How? Through learning the valuable art of dehypnotizing yourself from negativism.

Mr. D., a superb teacher, learned this art. He was working for his Ph.D. and chose sex in prison as the subject for his dissertation. He researched it thoroughly and then prepared to type it. It was then that he felt helpless. Repeatedly, he attempted to work on the second chapter, but it was futile. He could not seem to organize his thoughts and soon he had hypnotized himself into the conviction that he was incapable of doing it. Finally, in a noisy application of one of the cardinal rules of my theory of creative psycho-cybernetics, he hunted for the truth about himself. It was loud because he began screaming at himself things like "idiot" and "imbecile" and passersby undoubtedly questioned his sanity. Still, reflecting more quietly, he decided his second chapter was a stumbling block because he had not sufficiently mastered the subject matter. He decided that the proper course for him was to begin writing the other chapters. And, dehypnotized from the feeling that he was helpless to carry out this assignment, he buckled down to work and achieved his objective.

I, too, dehypnotized myself from this helplessness complex. Not only did I have to overcome a crisis of negativism as a student, which I've already related, but after graduation, when I rented an office on lower Fifth Avenue in New York City, I was hypnotized with an overpowering foreboding of failure. In two weeks, I received a telephone call from only one person, my mother. I was a nervous young plastic surgeon, pacing the floor glaring angrily at the telephone, hating it with a perverse passion. Finally, it would ring, and I would charge at it like a fullback pushing for a touchdown from the one-yard line. But it was only my mother.

By the third week of my patientless practice, I was gripped by desperation. I would gaze anxiously out the window watching construction of an apartment house across the street. A laborer high up almost tripped and fell. This triggered off fantasies that he would lose his balance and tumble, with resulting disfigurement of his face and newspaper headlines. By treating him, I would become famous overnight and thousands of patients would flock to my door. The aftermath of this fantasy was depressing. Not only did I feel paralyzed with futility, but my guilt over this morbid wish infected my spirit.

By the end of the third week, visions of disaster flooded my mind. The rent would be due soon; how could I pay it? I began to plan disposing of my office furniture, but realized it would not bring much. My silent feud with the telephone intensified and when, grudgingly, it finally rang, who do you think it was? Of course, my mother.

By the fourth week, I was mesmerized with failure feelings, I resumed pacing the floor. Again, the telephone rang. It was not my mother. It was a miracle, my first patient. At last, I was able to begin dehypnotizing myself from my visions of failure.

Suppose the phone had not rung. It would have been trying, but not fatal. Even though I did have some real financial problems, they were hypnotically exaggerated out of proportion, as when I feared the reactions of my classmates and professor. This created a process of negative hypnotism which I had to dispel.

Some time ago a teen-age girl swam the English Channel. She employed a positive form of hypnosis to bring her success in meeting the challenge. In an interview, she

71

confided that she had convinced herself that the icy water was mild; this belief helped her accomplish her goal.

This is positive hypnosis at its best. Most of us, however, need to dehypnotize ourselves of negative beliefs. How many salesmen see failure before they approach the customer? How many job applicants see rejection before the job interview? How many students see an F before they open a textbook? How many of us are umpires who call three strikes on ourselves before we even step up to the plate to swing?

Unfortunately, too many. You can throw away your black velvet cape, discard your top hat, and give away the rabbit under it. You don't need hypnosis; you need dehypnosis. This is the way to do it.

You start to dehypnotize yourself from undermining fictions about yourself when you stop trying to imitate other people. This form of overconformity is a desperate attempt of a person wallowing in an inferiority complex to escape the confines he has placed on himself.

Remember this: You are a distinct, unique individual brought into this world by our Creator to live meaningfully. Stop feeling that you must keep up with others. Feel satisfied when you keep up with yourself. Neither inferior nor superior, you are your unique self. When you see this, you are en route to dehypnotization from your inferiority complex.

Dehypnotization involves developing the habit of relaxing in the same way that you learned to wash your face or brush your teeth. In the sense that you must be able to rise above intolerable tension, this habit is equally basic. In the playhouse of your mind, a bright sunny room, a geyser erupting outside the window, symbolic of your need to release your stress and renew yourself for tomorrow's struggles. Techniques of relaxation are reminiscent of hypnosis because you focus on hidden powers to bring back mental pictures of past successes. This should give you peace of mind in the present. Hypnotize yourself toward the success habit; dehypnotize yourself from obsessive worry. That's the psycho-cybernetic way.

A basic ingredient of inferiority-complex dehypnotization is the invaluable art of winning friends. This is because you cannot feel unworthy when you retain the capacity for friendship.

Here are some sure-fire ways to make friends:

1. *Befriend yourself first.* You can't despise yourself and feel warm toward others. While it may be possible to downgrade yourself and still admire others, any positive feeling will be spoiled by envy. People around you, sensing the impurity of what you have to offer, will shrink from you. Understand that you are a product of Our Creator's love, that inside you are qualities of tenderness and compassion, even if you conceal them from the world and from yourself. Recall and reexperience the parts of yourself that you've always cherished, even if they are somewhat tainted by life's brutalizing influences.

2. *Recapture the simplicity of childhood.* In that part of your life, your attachments were naive, unsophisticated, pure, idealistic perhaps, but they were also spontaneous and refreshing, free of the pretensions and complex burdens of society.

3. *Concentrate on a reactivation of your affectionate nature.* Lose the taint of disillusion and slough off the poison of resentment. Hard as it may be, try to make a fresh start. Bathe your imagination with feelings of gratitude for an act of warmth on the part of a parent or a friend or, even more touching, a total stranger. Can you remember the gentle glow of birthday parties, the adoration you felt for toys or pets, the worship of now-fallen idols, the confiding talks with close friends? If your existence has been bleak, focus on those few instances in which you felt grateful to others. You see, gratitude is a soothing feeling which warms you like a

campfire and keeps alive your capacity for appreciation and love.

4. *Accept your imperfections.* When you do, you will grant comparable acceptance to the human frailties of others, and a tolerant attitude will make you indispensable to most embattled individuals on this insecure planet.

5. *Reach out toward others.* You will find their response more than gratifying. The trouble here is that so many people feel that they are unlovable. This is not so. Your lovability may be buried under layers of superficial defenses or mixed in with hostility and envy, but, though perhaps impure, it is there.

6. *Identify with the other fellow.* Put yourself in his shoes and reconstruct as best you can with limited knowledge his total life situation. Then you can empathize with his needs, and if he is a worthwhile person he will repay you with gratitude and loyalty.

7. *Be tolerant of the other's individuality.* He is not you; accept him as he is. Never force another person to conform to your preconceptions. Such domineering tactics will earn you only his rage and vindictiveness.

8. *Strive to satisfy the needs of others.* Try assuming as considerate an attitude toward their emotional growth as you would toward your own. Don't talk at people; talk to them—and, still better, listen.

Are you dehypnotized from your self-estrangement? Is liking for yourself beginning to appear, if only at the fringes of your thinking? Join the writer of this letter, and find your way to contentment.

Dear Doctor Maltz:

Thank you so much for writing your book, *Psycho-Cybernetics.* I just recently gave away my fifteenth copy of *Psycho-Cybernetics* in paperback. I find the hard-cover book makes a beautiful gift. It's my way of giving "you" rave notices.

My first encounter with your writings was strange. I was spending New Year's Eve alone and, as reading is one of my favorite pastimes, I looked for something to read to lose track of time. The back cover of your book, *Psycho-Cybernetics*, fascinated me. Buying it, I still went home feeling a little sorry for myself. You, my dear man, changed my life that very evening and at such a beautiful time of year.

My latest achievement took me ten months to accomplish and when it did materialize, the happiness I experienced—I must confess—brought tears to my eyes. And I have so many other things going for me it is unbelievable. Never again will I be bored or at a loss as to what life is all about.

Thank you sincerely,
Miss Leigh M. Dubay

GUIDELINES

1. Within us is the power to change our feelings of inferiority by dehypnotizing ourselves from negative beliefs.

2. We dehypnotize ourselves from false beliefs the moment we stop trying to be what we are not.

3. We dehypnotize ourselves when we stop trying to be superior in an effort to overcome an inferiority complex.

4. We must keep up with ourselves. We are neither superior nor inferior. We are as we are.

5. We dehypnotize ourselves from stresses by walking into the playhouse of our mind and seeing a geyser letting off steam.

6. We dehypnotize ourselves from extra unnecessary fears, extra unnecessary worry.

Principles to Live By

1. All habits represent daily forms of hypnosis.
2. Self-confidence is creative hypnosis.
3. Fear is negative hypnosis.

4. Negative beliefs are similar to absurd ideas implanted in the mind of a person by a professional hypnotist.

5. You begin to dehypnotize yourself from the poison of negative beliefs when you stop criticizing yourself and others, when you cease the noxious practice of "keeping up with the Joneses" and insist on keeping up only with yourself.

6. Hypnotically, with a positive approach, you can move toward success.

7. Follow the advice of Mark Twain and refuse to disown your illusions. If you obliterate them—your illusions, your dreams, your aspirations—you may lack the desire to follow through to rich living.

8. You must live in the present, trying to reach one goal at a time.

9. Your thinking must be productive, creative. Remember the words of John Dewey: "To me Faith means not worrying."

EXERCISE

Once again, in the playhouse of your mind, you sprawl out on the thick carpeting of this lush theater and, clasping your hands behind your head, you engage in a constructive dialogue with yourself.

"I came into this world to succeed, not to fail," you tell yourself, "and I am somebody. Yes, I am a person of worth. Every day I will work to intensify my faith in myself and with this faith I will soar to my destination. Negative feelings will bind my wings, preventing me from takeoff, and I must dehypnotize myself from their handicapping influence. I must understand that I was made in God's image to love my fellow man. I must learn to accept my imperfections and stop the damaging barrage of hostile, critical thoughts. I must harness the power of my compassion and courage so that I can stand up to stress. I must cast away the fear and resentment that hurl me into a dark dungeon of despair."

On a sheet of paper or on the mirror print the words "FAITH" and "BELIEF" in bold capital letters. Study them in your spare time because these are words to remember. Retain them in your mind with the same sense of urgency with which you would retain "rainy day" money in your savings account. Faith and belief may prove even more valuable.

Thoughts to Live By

1. *Frustration can be the beginning of self-fulfillment.* This is so because the person who is bogged down and immobilized has no choice but to fight his way out of the pit and into the sunlight.

2. *Every day will bring a better job.* Promotion, that's the key word. After dehypnotizing yourself, you promote better goals, better images, better techniques of action. Your entire life is getting better.

Chapter 5

Goal-Striving and Clear Creative Thinking

You will continue on the road to a happier life through application of my principles of creative psycho-cybernetics.

Your self-image will grow, your success mechanism will take over, your lifelong objectives will be realized. You cannot do this with confused incoherent thinking.

Intangible as it is, clear creative thinking is a basic skill you must master to function at your psycho-cybernetic best. Without it, you could be a rhinoceros or an elephant—and almost as clumsy.

The countdown now begins toward clear creative thinking, and once again, in the playhouse of our mind, we observe an unfolding drama.

CASE HISTORY

DOCTOR: How old are you, Rosalie?

ROSALIE: Thirty-eight.

DOCTOR: And what is your problem?

ROSALIE: I have a strange obsessive fear of water.

DOCTOR: Why?

ROSALIE: I don't really know. I tried to swim but I couldn't go through with it.

DOCTOR: When did this fear start?

ROSALIE: When I was ten, swimming, I wandered too far out into the lake. This was at a church party. I almost

78

drowned. At first, people didn't believe I was serious when I cried for help.

DOCTOR: But that was twenty-eight years ago.

ROSALIE: True, but there is nothing I can do about this fear.

DOCTOR: Sure you can. When I was six I was hurled into the river by other kids. I learned to swim. I had no choice.

ROSALIE: I wish I were like you.

DOCTOR: You are. But what do you like to do?

ROSALIE: Oh, I love to fly. I've been a stewardess for fifteen years.

DOCTOR: Married?

ROSALIE: For six years. I was divorced two years ago.

DOCTOR: Children.

ROSALIE: No.

DOCTOR: What was your husband's occupation?

ROSALIE: He was in the insurance business. He wanted a family immediately, but I wanted to remain a stewardess. We were not compatible.

DOCTOR: Do you have any other fears?

ROSALIE: Yes, I dread being alone.

DOCTOR: How about negative feelings?

ROSALIE: I'm a procrastinator.

DOCTOR: Why?

ROSALIE: I don't know. I start to take tennis lessons, then give up.

DOCTOR: Do you follow through with anything?

ROSALIE: I guess not.

DOCTOR: Are you happy as a stewardess after fifteen years?

ROSALIE: Oh, it's all right, but I'd rather get a license to sell real estate.

DOCTOR: Do you think you'd be good at it?

ROSALIE: Maybe I would be.

DOCTOR: Do you like yourself?

ROSALIE: Not really.

DOCTOR: Why not?

ROSALIE: I guess I wish I had more character. I don't seem to finish anything I start.

DOCTOR: Don't you follow through on any of your goals?

ROSALIE: I guess not.

DOCTOR: Why?

ROSALIE: I don't know. That's why I'm here.

DOCTOR: Have you any self-respect?

ROSALIE: Some, but not enough.

DOCTOR: Are you opinionated?

ROSALIE: No.

DOCTOR: Are you opinionated about yourself?

ROSALIE: Well, in a negative way.

DOCTOR: Are you in hiding?

ROSALIE: What do you mean?

DOCTOR: From yourself. What do you think of yourself?

ROSALIE: I am in envy of other people who do more with their lives.

DOCTOR: Tell me about your family.

ROSALIE: Mother was the dominant force. I admired her. Father was a laborer. He was always exhausted. Mother was better educated, and gave me more attention.

DOCTOR: What do you see when you look in the mirror?

ROSALIE: It varies. Sometimes I'm happy, sometimes displeased with myself.

DOCTOR: What would you like to become?

ROSALIE: Well, I'd like to marry again and perhaps sell real estate. I liked your book. Can you help me?

DOCTOR: You must help yourself.

ROSALIE: How?

DOCTOR: By coming to grips with your fear of drowning. By understanding why you procrastinate.

ROSALIE: Why do I?

DOCTOR: Procrastination for you means yesterday. You are no longer the little girl of ten who almost drowned. You must live in the present, twenty-eight years later.

ROSALIE: What should I do?

DOCTOR: You have read my book; that's not enough. You must live it, thinking clearly, creatively, in the present, ignoring past failures. You must decide *what* to do—

80

not what you don't want to do. Success means rising above past failures. Goal-oriented, creative ideas must replace old frustrated ideas. Play a new record, not the old record of yesterday. Why persist in this fear of water? Other people have overcome much more severe fears.

ROSALIE: Where do I start?

DOCTOR: Here's a little mental exercise. Go to a mirror and with your lipstick write from above downward these three words: "Drown"—"Swim"—"Survive." Now the point is you didn't drown. You're alive. You must live in the now, not in yesterday. Sixty percent of what you see in the mirror is yesterday. The fact that you could not swim then doesn't mean you can't swim now. I feel you must learn to swim; this is your most important goal. You can achieve this goal. One failure doesn't make you a failure for life. If you learn to swim, you will give up the fright and heartache of yesterday. Swimming is symbolic of surviving and of reaching a goal and of deprocrastinating. As a stewardess, haven't you been flying away from reality? Learn how to swim and reach port. You must reach one successful goal before you can reach other goals. Give yourself a chance, you deserve it. You can become your big self if you try.

[NARRATOR: The doctor saw Rosalie a year later. She had learned to swim and was radiant. She had passed the examination for her real estate license. She had found a new side of herself. Her thinking was clear and creative, and she hoped someday to meet the right man.]

HOMEWORK

Practice the process of switching your thinking from failure to success.

Typical examples of thought-switching:

I brooded over a blunder made years ago, but switched to my current business achievements and did not mull over the old mistake.

On a gloomy, rainy morning, I began to bury myself in gloomy thoughts, but I pulled up short and began to think about how lucky I am to be healthy, alive, loved. All of a sudden, I found myself singing and whistling.

I found myself condemning an old friend for a slurring remark I was told he made about me. Switching to positive thinking, I tracked down the rumor, found it was not true, and saved a cherished friendship.

As a child, I was told I was too clumsy to dance. For years, I believed this, and never danced. Recently I took lessons, and now I'm a better-than-average hoofer.

Since birth, I was taught not to associate with a certain race of "inferior" people. In the past week, I cultivated the acquaintance of several members of this race; I find them worthwhile.

QUESTIONS AND ANSWERS

Q. To change negative beliefs, feelings or behavior, must a person dredge up material from what Freudians term the "unconscious"?

A. Our power of rational, logical thinking can not only change conscious factors, but can also change the "unconscious."

Q. What is the "unconscious" called in psycho-cybernetics?

A. The automatic mechanism.

Q. Does this mechanism have a will of its own?

A. It is impersonal, working solely upon the data we feed it. Change the data and you change the mechanism.

Q. What is the "control knob" of this automatic mechanism?

A. Conscious thinking.

Q. Is there merit in digging around in the past?

A. No. We must start in the present.

Q. What produces enjoyment?

82

A. Learning to control your current thinking.

Q. What about "Let sleeping dogs lie"?

A. Memories of past failures are not harmful so long as your conscious attention is focused on present positive goals.

Q. What if we dwell upon past errors and guilts?

A. These are yesterday's "goals" and your imagination becomes chained to failure instead of feeling free to work toward today's goals for success.

Q. How can we live now instead of reliving yesterday?

A. We can change our minds and stop giving power to the past. Then the mistakes of yesterday lose their power over us.

Q. How does hypnosis prove that yesterday has no power over us if we change our minds?

A. Under hypnosis, we act as we believe. If our conviction is contrary to our past conduct, we change to present belief.

Q. How does hypnosis release talents, capabilities, and powers?

A. Memories of past failures are blocked off during hypnosis. When the hypnotist orders us to do certain things, we do not fear failure and we do them.

Q. Why can't we use these powers without hypnosis?

A. Worrying over former failures convinces us we will fail again and that it is futile to try.

Q. How is it possible to ignore prior failures and to act as if we cannot fail?

A. By assuming that the power is there for us to use.

Q. How do we rid ourselves of illogical guilt feelings?

A. By convincing ourselves that they are ridiculous. Recognizing their irrationality, we can pull them out by the roots and reject them. Outdated guilt feelings are not consistent with our new self-image.

Q. What is the next step after purging ourselves of ancient guilts?

A. Feel emphatic about what you now believe and live according to your new convictions. Never permit irrational ideas to gain a foothold in your mind.

Q. Why is a clear self-image important?

A. Automatically, we accept ideas based upon deeply held beliefs, rejecting inconsistent concepts. Why are ideas not changed by our willpower? Because they are changed by other ideas. Negative concepts are replaced by ideas consistent with our beliefs.

Q. How can you reevaluate ideas that you are undeserving and inferior, that others are hostile, and that the world is an unfriendly dangerous arena?

A. Ask yourself
   1. Why do you cling to these beliefs?
   2. Are there rational reasons for it?
   3. Would you reach the same conclusion if another person believed this?
   4. Why continue to believe what is not really truth?

Q. When should we take a hard look at our beliefs?

A. When we find ourselves manipulated and destroyed by negative habits.

Q. What will make clear creative thinking effective?

A. Deep desire and enthusiasm.

Q. How does clear creative thought resemble worry?

A. Both involve imagination, but, worrying, we imagine a negative end result. Clear creative thought envisions a positive result.

Q. How does one use his automatic mechanism for success or failure?

A. This depends upon the data and objectives we supply. Success or failure is determined by the caliber of our input into the mechanism.

Q. Does the mechanism sort out the data?

A. No, it operates upon all data.

Q. What about rejection of inconsistent ideas?

A. Rejection is by the conscious mind. If your conscious mind accepts data, your mechanism also accepts it.

Q. How critical must we be in accepting new facts?

A. We must try to understand the truth and to make rational evaluations.

Q. What about overestimating and underestimating?

A. Usually, we overestimate our difficulties and underestimate our capacities.

Q. What happens when a major goal is not achieved and we begin to focus on all the failure alternatives?

A. More thought goes into failure alternatives than into success options and this usually predetermines failure.

Q. Why must we trust the automatic mechanism?

A. Because even though clear creative thought selects the goal, gathers the data, concludes, estimates, and causes the mechanism to function, it is not responsible for the results. We must lay the groundwork, act upon sensible assumptions, and leave final results for the mechanism to handle.

The Crisp Scenario of You

Now back to the playhouse of your mind, an amphitheater of glistening, scintillating possibilities in which a marvelous scenario unfolds. It is an inspiring chronicle, a passionate success story, a happy consummation of potential, an exciting, dramatic unearthing of a precious buried treasure that has lain hidden too long.

Your digging tool? Clear creative thinking.

Your product? The supreme emotional enjoyment that your spirit is capable of yielding up: peace of mind, fulfillment, self-respect, an enriching capacity for dynamic creative living in the finest qualitative sense.

No more fantasies for you, no more daydreams. You can bank on the solid foundation of reality and on the clear formulation of worthwhile objectives. Additionally, you are going to bank on the health of your self-image and on the sure-handed reactivation of the cool, searing fire of your success mechanism.

You won't anticipate a supernatural intervention in your behalf because life has taught you the need for depending upon yourself. You must refuse to delude yourself. Your strength will come from the logical, rational, probing nature of your thinking. With this potent weapon, you will charge irrepressibly upon your goals.

Overwhelmed by today's technology, inundated by materialistic pressures, too many people have lost sight of the incalculable value of clear thinking. This loss is tragic; don't let it be yours.

Clear creative thinking, along with its allied elements, is your basis for growth as a human being. In your private laboratory of the playhouse of your mind, you synthesize your creative thoughts from the raw materials. You screen out the distracting commotion around you to intensify your rationality. You then channel your prime-quality thoughts into constructive goal-oriented actions. Achievement feeds your confidence, reactivates the functioning of your success mechanism, builds your self-image, and fortifies you to survive chaos and uncertainty. You will rise above all doubt and fear and make an unshakable investment in yourself and your future.

"Success story," you say, "buried treasure." This may sound like extravagant language. Agreed, I am somewhat of a ham, *but* I mean every word I say. These internal factors are just as dramatically crucial to your happiness as I tell you they are. Nothing is more basic than clear creative thinking and the other interrelated emotional-mental concepts I stress.

Remember this while you are working to build the foundation of your life: You can bank on money, and then lose it. You can count on a friend, and he can prove disloyal. You can stake everything on property, and disintegrate as it depreciates in value.

But if, stone by stone, you build a foundation of clear creative thinking, goal-oriented and self-image–enhancing, and if you strengthen it every day with will-power and real desire, that foundation will support you while others around you with weaker values fall. Sure, you might possibly lose your mind too. But you can combat this through the playhouse of your mind. You can win the battle against negative feelings. With a good self-image, you can retake territory that is rightfully yours but which you surrendered through negative thinking and negative doing.

You are still whole. With clear creative thinking, you can win through.

Desire is your takeoff point. But this should involve no problem at all because once you have arrived at a full realization of the underlying significance of your thinking, you will never neglect its development.

Impetuous action in a life of complexities may be disastrous. You must not rush heedlessly into overt action. First, you should ponder, weigh, and assess.

Polishing your furniture or your floor or your car reflects your concern. Your supreme concern now must be with polishing the character of your thinking.

Focus your reserves of energy upon dusting off, polishing, and realigning your thinking. No matter how busy you are, you have time for it. Each day, escape from the hue and cry around you. Insulate yourself in the playhouse of your mind and work to refresh the clarity and vitality of your thinking. Make this a daily habit, for it is most important for constructive living. Ward off intrusions every day so that you can concentrate on your thought processes. If your environment is noisy, find some soothing music and blot it out. If your phone rings incessantly, adjust it so the ring doesn't jangle your nerves.

Control the atmosphere around you as best you can, and then go to it. Think. Think to win.

You must make yourself aware of your hidden resources. You may not know it, but they exist. The trouble is, few people really tap them. In my lifetime, I have heard many a human being discarded offhandedly as a "drunk," a "bum," a "crackpot," and so on, as if an epithet, degrading and unjust, could faithfully characterize a human being. Because of the nature of my lifework, I have seen many people in distraught, defeated, hysterical, and enraged conditions, and I must say this: I have never met a "hopeless" person. The tragedy is that the pace of living is so fast and life's complexities are so staggering that when someone gets into difficulty and needs help straightening himself out, others are too anxious or too busy or too exhausted to lend a helping hand. Thus, many people drown who might have been given artificial respiration and been saved.

This underlines the importance of what I have already said: You must learn to rely on yourself and on the development of your capacity for clear creative thinking.

Self-discipline is basic. This quality is discredited by many people today as "old-fashioned," but it is really extremely important. Remember, you must impose structure on your thinking, so that you will know where you're going and can make yourself aware of the limitations and boundaries as well as the possibilities of your specific objectives.

Create a stronger flow to your success thinking. In the playhouse of your mind you are onstage. Visualize great success pictures of yourself. Forget the images of past failures and heartbreaks. Feed your mind with the nourishing broth and the steaming sweet chocolate of your richest moments. See past successes again and again in your mind, and breathe enthusiasm and energy into your great automatic servomechanism.

The drama that is unfolding must have a direction; it

must move forward. Clear, creative, rational thinking prepares you for the challenge. You must gear yourself to sidestep the dangers of mental blackout and concentration on trivia and you will bring your reasoning faculties to their highest peak. Millions of thoughts and images may infiltrate the recesses of your mind. You must develop a sound screening process to weed out irrelevance; you must mass your energies in pursuit of basic goals.

Your search is for self-fulfillment, through the clarity and quality of your thinking.

This is where you will win the battle—in the playhouse of your mind.

Emulate Mr. Reuter of Chicago, who sent me this letter in the summer of 1972:

Dear Dr. Maltz:

Psycho-Cybernetics literally saved my life. I was an alcoholic for twenty years and had tried psychiatry, a superficial investigation of religion, AA, and many things to stop. Nothing worked. Doing your self-image exercises for over a year, thinking rationally and productively and making a spiritual commitment, did the trick. I quit drinking five years ago. I feel the combination of your book and the commitment enabled me to stop on my own, a source of wonder to AA members I talk to. Thank you, thank you for your book.

Your principles also enabled me to overcome ten years of chain-smoking and a thirty-year fear of water caused by a childhood diving accident. I now swim four strokes and dive, a constant source of joy and wonder to me each time I do so. Thank you, thank you for your loving book. I've given away about a hundred copies and plan to keep doing so.

Bless you good,
Ken Reuter

GUIDELINES

1. Concentrate on your thinking. When distractions invade your mind, when negative feelings threaten you, fight them off as you would a bee about to sting you.

2. Clear thinking starts with longing for improvement.

3. You build a better self-image from past successes— an image you can live with.

4. You do not think clearly without empathy for others.

5. Your own aspirations influence the aspirations of others.

6. You think creatively when you are not frustrated and fearful and are more in command of reality.

7. The emphasis on the search for self-fulfillment is on *you*.

8. The business of living is rising above a blunder, a misfortune.

Principles to Live By

1. Use your imagination creatively to build your true self-image and pave the way for clear thinking.

2. Creative thinking means discipline to live in the present.

3. Self-respect is the heartbeat of creative thinking.

4. Creative thinking requires that you build faith in yourself every day.

5. In clear thinking, in purposeful doing, you grow and reach out to self-fulfillment.

6. When you relax, you create the climate in your mind which will allow creative thinking to live and thrive.

7. Creative thinking means that you must continually search for the BIG you. You must help yourself become the person you want to be.

8. Accepting yourself not only as you are but as you can become—the better you—is your great enterprise.

9. Clear thinking means unearthing the hidden resources within you.

10. Think—and *do!* When? *NOW!*

EXERCISE

Once again, relax in the playhouse of your mind. A state of tranquillity is essential to clear thinking for, obviously, such thinking cannot coexist with tension and frustration.

Calmly, print on a sheet of paper the word "THINK" or block it out on the bathroom mirror with lipstick or crayon. "Think": study the word and analyze its importance. It assumes an identity like a life force, rising from symbolic neutrality to real significance.

"To fulfill myself," you muse "I must bank on the rational, creative potential of my thinking. I must focus prime attention on the vague yet powerful character of my thought formation. With dedication, I must probe within myself for the hidden assets that constitute my uniqueness. Seeking lost confidence, destroyed courage, I must strive to recapture these assets and use them to bolster my growing strength. I comprehend the supreme value of clear creative thinking and wish to harness it for fulfillment not only of my personal needs, but for the needs of others. In the playhouse of my mind, in the laboratory of my mind, I must transform the crude raw material of thought into action, delivering a splendid performance in pursuit of a cherished goal. I must resolve to keep my eye on the ball until I hit a home run and cross the plate."

Write on paper or mirror the words "DO" and "NOW." Then reflect further. "Thinking is not enough," you must tell yourself, "psycho-cybernetics means doing. When?

Now. Turning a creative thought into a creative performance. This shall be my daily objective."

Thoughts to Live By

1. *As a human being thinks, so shall he become.* This is guaranteed, if his thinking is clear and creative and if his goals are sharply defined.

2. *Your most rewarding competition is with yourself.* Battling the Joneses or the Smiths is a dead end. When you do this, you are defeating yourself because you are accepting their rules and playing on their ball field. Self-improvement is the name of the truly satisfying game, and your primary objective is to strengthen yourself, not to destroy an opponent.

Your Thinking: "Under New Management"

A word in closing this vital chapter: If your thinking has failed you over and over, do not despair. With effort, with determination, you can change.

Clear creative thinking is not easy—but it is certainly possible.

Did you ever take a walk through a business street, packed with stores, and note a drastic surprising change? The novelty store, drab and unappealing, almost barren of customers, showed a startling transformation. It became a stationery store, with neatly stacked piles of paper supplies and briefcases and typewriters and office machines. The clerks looked neat and were dynamic, the emporium bustled with customers and the continual ring of the cash register gave off a happy sound.

Glancing up, you saw a sign "UNDER NEW MANAGEMENT." Of course.

Still, you felt shocked. You had experienced expectation; yet the improvement had not erased the surprise in your reaction. Initially, the change was difficult to absorb.

Change is always somewhat shocking, but the thing to remember is that it is possible and very helpful.

So the store is "Under New Management." But what about your personal thinking processes?

If there is a need for "new management" there, make the painful change. It may be rough going at first, but it will be thoroughly worthwhile.

Work constantly to refine your mind powers and streamline your thinking into clear creative channels. This is your great opportunity to turn possibility into actuality—through the power of your mind.

Chapter 6

Relaxation Means Success

Another basic ingredient in your battle for the good life is relaxation. Indeed, success without relaxation is no success at all. It is a display, an exhibition, a substanceless impersonation.

Material success is fine, so are vocational achievement, military prowess, athletic skills, and personal accomplishment. Without inner peace, however, success is not real. The truly satisfied individual feels success in his bloodstream, and is able to relax.

To visualize the picture more completely, let's start off with another dramatization. You're seated in the playhouse of your mind. Are the house lights dim? Fine. Now the curtain rises.

CASE HISTORY

DOCTOR: What is your name?

MAN: Bill.

DOCTOR: How old are you?

BILL: Twenty-one. I'm a sophomore at a Southern university.

DOCTOR: Your problem?

BILL: I read your book *Psycho-Cybernetics* and tried working with it. My main problem, I'm always tense; I don't know how to relax.

DOCTOR: Why do you think you're so tense?

BILL: It bugs me. It's mostly in social situations. In high

school, I was very backward socially and this affected my work in school and my life in general.

DOCTOR: What do you mean by tense socially?

BILL: I haven't gone out much with girls.

DOCTOR: Have you dated *any* girls?

BILL: Some.

DOCTOR: Sexual intercourse?

BILL: No.

DOCTOR: Any brothers?

BILL: No. An older sister. She's a nurse in a hospital.

DOCTOR: Your parents, are they alive?

BILL: Yes, but separated.

DOCTOR: How did you get along with your father?

BILL: Pretty well. And I get along with my mother. I lived with her this summer.

DOCTOR: Do you care for men?

BILL: No.

DOCTOR: Were you tense as a child?

BILL: No.

DOCTOR: When did this tension take hold?

BILL: In eighth and ninth grade and in high school—from the age of thirteen.

DOCTOR: How did it start?

BILL: I felt socially inferior, I guess.

DOCTOR: And what do you think of yourself?

BILL: Sometimes I feel I'm okay, but then I'm not sure. I get upset by little things. I can't relax.

DOCTOR: Are you a perfectionist?

BILL: Yes.

DOCTOR: No one is perfect. Do you know this?

BILL: Well yes, but I guess I don't really believe it. I ask a girl out and if she has a bad time, I kick myself. I'm so ashamed.

DOCTOR: Do you feel defensive before you go out?

BILL: Yes.

DOCTOR: What else about your tension?

95

BILL: The main thing is I'm tense with girls. That's my problem.

DOCTOR: You think that's the real problem?

BILL: I'm afraid to go out with girls; I admit it.

DOCTOR: Camus, the French philosopher, said that greatness consists in trying to be great, success consists in trying to be successful, and friendship consists in trying to be a friend to someone. Do you believe that?

BILL: Yes.

DOCTOR: Who's the best friend you could have?

BILL: A steady girl friend.

DOCTOR: No other possibility? Take another guess.

BILL: I can't think of anybody.

DOCTOR: Think about yourself. You can't be a friend to others unless you're a friend to yourself.

BILL: How do you befriend yourself?

DOCTOR: By realizing that you are an important, unique person, different from any other human being, with fingerprints of your own. You are neither superior nor inferior. You have a right to succeed. You have the right to uncover the buried treasure within you.

BILL: Where do I start?

DOCTOR: First, don't expect people to fawn over you. It is your job to meet them halfway. How? Take the case of this girl. Go out of your way to be considerate.

BILL: How?

DOCTOR: Try to make her comfortable in your presence. If you give the nice relaxed part of yourself to others, baby, you'll get it back.

BILL: I never thought of that.

DOCTOR: Get off the fence and take your chances in life. No one can make you tense without your consent. You must learn to disinhibit yourself. You're an attractive young man, but your tension defeats you. Stop criticizing yourself, and see yourself at your best. Forgive yourself for your mistakes. Make it your business to be attentive to a girl's needs, encouraging her to be herself, and you'll encourage yourself to be the new you, free of tension. Your two most important bywords, what are they going to be?

BILL: Try?

DOCTOR: Yes, and what's the other?

BILL: I don't know.

DOCTOR: Relax. You overcome tension by forgiving yourself and forgiving others. You overcome your fear of making friends with a girl by trying. And you try creatively by giving the best in you. You wouldn't try to make friends with her by gritting your teeth, clenching your fists, and frowning. The business of living successfully is not letting tensions overpower you. Learn to take pride in yourself. Accept yourself and then impart your sense of worth to her. See yourself with kind eyes and you'll relax.

BILL: I'm listening, Doctor.

DOCTOR: Fine, but that is not enough. Turn your insight into a creative performance. Do one constructive thing at a time.

[NARRATOR: Bill visits the doctor six months later. A change is apparent.]

DOCTOR: Well?

BILL: I'm still somewhat tense.

DOCTOR: How much is somewhat?

BILL: I'm getting over it a little. When I date a girl I think of being nice to her and forget about my problems. I do feel calmer.

DOCTOR: You think you'll make it?

BILL: In time, yes. I understand now that I must do the job, in the present. I must let my success mechanism work for me by concentrating on a strong self-image, betting on myself. My tension gradually is lessening.

DOCTOR: I can see and feel that you are changing. I congratulate you.

BILL: There's one girl in particular. I'm excited, and yet I'm relaxed.

Discuss a personal form of thought control, by which you discarded an irrational concept because it was inconsistent; accepted one because it was consistent; or weeded out an outdated belief because you were aware it was not consistent with building your self-image.

Typical examples of thought control:

Desire to take a flyer in the stock market was rejected as not consistent with my need for secure savings. Accepted a compromise, moving savings from bank to building-and-loan, increasing interest without losing security. Rooted out deep conviction that only commercial banks were safe places for savings.

Idea of making a pass at another woman was discarded as inconsistent with sincere affection for my wife. Perhaps guilt arising from this impulse prompted the thought that I would demonstrate my affection by buying her a dishwasher she had long cherished. I changed my old Romeo/wolf complex which was not consistent with my new image as a loyal husband.

Rejected the urge for a second helping as inconsistent with need for diet control. Accepted the concept that more exercise would be consistent with diet control. Also rejected conviction held since childhood that huge meals were beneficial to health.

Rooted out the fantasy of a stereotyped world cruise as inconsistent with my goal of making the acquaintance of people from other countries in a real sense. Accepted the concept of studying foreign languages and cycling through out-of-the-way provinces. Weeded out the outdated belief that I'm too old for such activities.

Rooted out an obsessive need to write psychological novels as inconsistent with a limited knowledge of people. Accepted the truth that I need greater higher-quality involvement with others. Rejected the blanket idea that I cannot write, replacing it with the more specific idea that I can't write psychological novels *at this time*.

Rejected the feeling that people avoid me because I am unworthy, since this is inconsistent with my new self-image. Accepted the thought that I've avoided other people. Worked to remove these old ideas of unworthiness, substituting vivid images of worthwhile conduct.

Rejected the idea of tuning out someone whose beliefs were inconsistent with my self-image. Accepted the notion that I might still learn from such a person.

Stopped myself in the middle of a house-selling transaction because of panic. Realized that the panicky feelings were generated by gloomy associates. This was inconsistent with my new self-image of self-control and, realizing this, the panic vanished.

QUESTIONS AND ANSWERS

Q. Why do we suffer from stress, ulcers, worry?

A. We try to solve our problems by conscious forebrain thinking.

Q. What are the functions of the forebrain?

A. It formulates goals, gathers information, makes observations, evaluates data, forms judgments.

Q. What are the limitations of the forebrain?

A. It cannot create or do the job. It can pose and identify problems, but is not designed to solve problems.

Q. What if we rely almost exclusively on the forebrain?

A. We become overcautious.

Q. What kind of drivers would we be if we used only the forebrain?

A. Poor. We could not cope simultaneously with all the problems.

Q. Is the philosophy "You can't be too careful" risky?

A. It is riskier to creep onto a freeway than to accelerate onto it at better than fifty miles an hour.

Q. We have utilized the forebrain to make a decision. Now what happens?

A. Dismiss all concern about the outcome. Unclamp your mental machinery.

Q. Is there victory through surrender?

A. Yes. Give up the battle to solve problems by conscious thought; reactivate the functioning of your success mechanism, abandon convulsiveness, and find your greater self.

Q. What do writers, inventors, and other creators tell us about the creative process?

A. Creative ideas do not arise consciously, but automatically and spontaneously. You cannot force creativity.

Q. What is the initial prerequisite for creative thinking?

A. Conscious definition of your problem and consideration of possible courses of action, along with an intense desire and a vivid visualization of your goal.

Q. Then what?

A. Additional straining and fretting will not help and may hinder.

Q. Do we have to be Edisons or Shakespeares to feel creative?

A. We are all potentially creative, but we pursue different courses of creativity.

Q. What is creative performance?

A. A strong, spontaneous, natural, relaxed force lets the task do itself through us.

Q. What is the meaning of "inhibited"?

A. Held back. Being too consciously concerned and anxious about doing the right thing; calculating every statement and action for its effect rather than for its purpose.

Q. How do we liberate our creative machinery from the limitations of inhibition?

A. Live now; do one thing at a time; learn to relax.

Q. What distinction is there between long-range planning and living in tomorrow?

A. Planning for tomorrow is fine, but we must not live in it.

Q. How do we define creative living?

A. Reacting spontaneously to environment, to what is happening now, not to what might be.

Q. What formula helps us feel alive now?

A. Alertness to our sensory impressions; awareness of the quality of interactions with people, not to what they say, but to what they mean.

Q. How can we stop stewing about tomorrow or yesterday?

A. Ask yourself what you should respond to *here* and *now*.

Q. What provokes nervousness?

A. Trying to do something impossible for today, reacting to fiction, not reality; jumping to the conclusion that a present person or situation is identical with a person or situation that was troublesome in the past.

Q. Can we think of more than one thing at a time?

A. Not well. We can really do justice to only one thing at a time, although simultaneously we can make many habitual responses.

Q. How do you get results by "sleeping on" a problem?

A. Make a conscious effort to define the problem or envision the objective before going to sleep.

Q. Is it negative to relax at work?

A. No. Relaxation from time to time reduces fatigue and improves one's ability to handle tough situations by eliminating excessive tension.

The Magic in Relaxation

From dramatization to homework assignment to questions and answers, we travel and travel again the twin worlds of tension and tranquillity: one world is abrasive and irritating; the other is a land of inner calm.

There is a magic in relaxation; it is music with a soothing tone. Unfortunately, today's world does not seem to produce this calming quality in many individuals. For that matter, is there any historical epoch in which the so-called "average person" basked in peaceful serenity? If there was, I cannot recall having read or heard about it.

In our materialistic, technological civilization, in which money and consumer goods are yardsticks with most people, we cannot gain inner peace through accumulation of possessions. Tranquillity will not flow through your body because you own a car or two cars or a house or a country estate or a chain of hotels; your bruised spirit will not be eased because you rent a penthouse or own a condominium or wear fur coats and diamond rings.

You nod your head knowingly. "Then you admit," you say, "that tranquillity does not exist."

On the contrary, I insist that almost anyone can attain the privileged state of relaxation, but not through material possessions alone. The blessed sanctuary of your mind is the battlefield on which you fight for your right to genuine peace.

The big trouble is that meditation and quiet and relaxation are lost arts in our fast-moving jet-age culture. They survive in some parts of the Orient, but twentieth-century Western civilization seethes with tension-hounded people making a buck, moving onward, climbing up the ladder, maintaining surface poise. Underneath, however, a quiescent volcano is ready to erupt.

This may be an age of affluence and material comfort,

but it is also an age of migraine headaches, ulcers, sleeping pills, and "social drinkers." In the famous words of the philosopher Henry David Thoreau, a big winner in the solitude of Walden Pond, "Most men live lives of quiet desperation."

Therefore, you must seek a composite, comprehensive, all-inclusive type of success, which includes the ability to relax in your spare time and which cuts down the chance of death from heart attack in your forties or fifties.

You are onstage now in the playhouse of your mind; evaluate your performance.

Do you see tension? Are your facial muscles twitching, is your forehead creased in lines, your mouth clenched and your chin tight? Is your voice weak and unsteady? Do you fidget, a mass of jangling nerves, shuffling your feet, moving your hands around nervously? Is this the image you love to view in the playhouse of your mind?

Of course not! But how can you rise above tension to reclaim your identity as a whole, successful human being?

A giant step is to focus on the basic source of your difficulties, not your physical tone but the underlying disturbances in your mind.

Do you judge your failures with an overdose of harshness? Try to temper self-criticism with kindness and respect. It might help if you took a long look at the human frailties of other people; if you can accept other people's weaknesses, surely you can tolerate your own.

One process that will help you to relax is developing a feeling that you possess human rights. This may sound strange. Doesn't everyone, after all, have rights? In truth, many people do not *feel* this. They may have responsibilities, heartaches, deprivations—but no rights. Bring reasonable expectations into balance and write a personal commitment to yourself.

Another tension-easing factor is the ability to set real-istic limits. Shoot for the moon if you wish, but learn to settle for satisfying goals on earth.

Easing the tensions of others will help you relax. Why? Because relaxation is contagious. It is communicable, but offers no preventive inoculation. Paint the day in lovely colors for a friend, and you will find the glow lingering in your heart.

In sleep, also, you will find refreshment to relax your world-weary soul. Remember, however, that you can't force sleep; you can organize a climate in which sleep comes over you in waves. Then you must leave the rest to your great automatic servomechanism.

Here are some additional rules for relaxation:

1. *Stop holding grudges.* When you nurture grievances in your mind and heart, your vindictive attitude mostly injures you. You poison yourself with inner tension and reel with dizziness from hostility.

Forgiveness, that's the ticket. Forgiveness places you on the road to relaxation. When you cancel out an ancient grudge, forgiving your enemy and wiping the slate clean, your gracious sensible orientation is heart-warming to the other person but the chief beneficiary is you. Forgiveness clears your bloodstream, opens up your physical tone, grants you the capacity to bask freely in the sunshine.

Is that all? No! Forgiving others is great; but still more basic is to forgive yourself. Wipe your own slate clean of past errors, erring judgments, and negative motivation, so that you can relax in the most complete sense, apply-ing a soothing balm to your own wounds.

2. *Learn to look at things from the other fellow's point of view.* If you put yourself in his shoes, you will feel less vulnerable to chronic resentment, one of the main peace-of-mind killers.

3. *Every day take stock of your assets.* Obsession with

liabilities is another relaxation-destroyer. Count what is on the good side of the ledger.

4. *Remember the glowing feel of past successes.* Nothing is more relaxing than happy memories. Bury the gaunt ghost of past mistakes; invigorate your spirit with reminiscences that make you proud of yourself.

5. *Do not run away from yourself.* Instead, walk with dignity, even in troubled times, and relax with reality. Crisis is a time when the weak hide and the strong stand their ground.

6. *Envision a geyser outside the playhouse of your mind.* It lets off steam as you watch, and the meaning is of course symbolic. You are a human being, not a god. An occasional release, a geyser within you that erupts, helps you return to yourself, more relaxed, ready to renew faith in yourself and your goals.

The following letter was written by a male student in a Miami, Florida, class in psycho-cybernetics.

What I think of myself is predicated on who I am and what I am in day-to-day activity in life. Today I have an opinion of myself unlike that of previous years. I am more realistic about my basic beliefs of my actual existence, which is God-given. At this point I am able to reconstruct my thoughts with respect to my activities in my life. It is important for me to form the best and the highest possible attainment of my particular talents and to pursue these with vigor and well-being.

I feel presently that I have not obtained these objectives due to the emotional scars inflicted on me by myself and allowing others this unrightful privilege. But I see many possibilities for rapid and successful growth and through inventory.

Full realization of the negative aspects coped with knowledge and action . . . to know that relaxation is nature's tranquillizer to overcome tension . . . to remember what Dr. Maltz says . . . that we all have a built-in spiritual thermostat which enables us to maintain an emotional climate and atmosphere despite the emotional weather around us. All this I am sure will produce results. I know I am going to let my success mechanism work for me. One goal at a time. A goal I will reach.

Yes, *I like me*. After all, *I'm all I've got.*

And here is a letter from a married woman in New York State.

Dear Dr. Maltz:

Thank you for your book *Psycho-Cybernetics*. Read it a lot and often think of you during the day. When things get tough, I say: "Oh Max!" And then I stand up to the tension and stress and relax. Isn't that funny? But I knew you'd understand and enjoy hearing how you help.

> Sincerely,
> *Mrs. C. F.*

GUIDELINES

1. A clenched fist means tension. An open hand means relaxation.

2. A frown means tension; a smile, relaxation.

3. Accept other people's weaknesses and you will tolerate your own.

4. You have a right to tranquillity. Assert this right.

5. Stand up with resolution to the tensions of the day, refusing to permit them to overpower you.

6. Live in the NOW, remembering that it is just as easy to develop a good habit of relaxation as a bad habit of despair.

7. See yourself at your best as a person of confidence, not at your worst as a person of frustration.

Principles to Live By

1. Two important goals for you. Forgive others. Forgive yourself. Set all your goals within your personal limitations, within your training and capabilities.

2. A proper self-image means relaxation.

3. Relaxation is an active, full-time job. Search for the better you, a daily enterprise as long as you live.

4. Every day is a day for daily growth.

5. Adjust to the realities of the day. Separate fact from fancy.

6. Don't downgrade yourself.

7. You will never be happy and relaxed if you spend your time trying to be someone else. Accept yourself for what you are.

8. You move toward relaxation when you feel big enough to make peace with your human failings. Don't hide behind deception.

9. Learn this basic truth. Relaxation is a great opportunity that you create for yourself.

EXERCISE

Every day for six days stare at the image of you in the mirror. Watch your face in tension. Your forehead is wrinkled, your teeth are clenched, you bite your lip, and your fists are squeezed into tight balls.

Direct your conversation to the image in the mirror:

"Look, friend, your assignment is to rise above tension to relaxation. Bury your troubles in the tomb of time and gather your forces. Tell yourself that you were made in God's image, destined to succeed and give meaning to your life, so that you will not fail."

Turn away from the mirror, discarding your worried look while pivoting. Then do an about-face and see yourself once again in the mirror. This time a smile of confidence should grace your face.

You must see this image not only in the looking glass, but in the playhouse of your mind.

In times of stress, let this serve as a symbol for you to call upon your powers of relaxation to help you survive with dignity and self-respect.

Thoughts to Live By

1. *Relaxation is Nature's tranquillizer.* You must purge yourself of tension and trouble and relax, no matter how difficult your reality.

2. *Relaxation means total immersion in today.* You must escape the catastrophes of the past and the uncertainties of the future. Living today, dynamically and creatively, you can do your best to reach worthwhile goals. Then, relax.

Inner Peace: Our Lucky Charm

Recently, I finished writing an historical novel dealing with sixteenth-century Italy. That was indeed an intensely superstitious age and during that period the common people, ignorant and terrified, tried to protect themselves from unseen dangers by wearing on their persons amulets of a compound called theriac, made largely of the flesh of vipers and prepared under circumstances that we today would have to regard as ludicrous. These amulets of theriac, like the more contemporary rabbit's foot, were reputedly "good-luck charms," preventives of the dread plague and so on, and, wearing these absurd contraptions, the populace was able to surmount anxiety and relax.

Yes, relaxation is basic; but, fortunately, today you do not need such nonsense to arrive at a state of inner peace. Common sense with imagination, intelligence, and awareness: these are the ingredients of my "compound" to help you attain peace of mind in an age of anxiety.

These ingredients will work for you—if you work for them.

Chapter 7

The Automatic Happiness Mechanism

Your most vital ally in your search for richer, fuller, truly meaningful living is the great automatic servo-mechanism inside you. But the key question is: Do you use this as a happiness mechanism or as a device for self-annihilation?

Obviously, your hope is for happiness, but how do you go about it? In this chapter we will explore possibilities of an inspiring inner revolution, in which we will seek to cast out the twin poisons of self-doubt and despair, replacing them with renewed self-trust and determination. We will strive to reactivate faith in our powers and our possibilities, formulating objectives for which we can feel genuine enthusiasm and moving toward them.

In other words, we will gear our every effort toward enlisting the aid of our automatic mechanism as a happiness mechanism. Our essential preparation will take place in the inner space of our mind, and in this prolific playhouse we now view the following dramatization.

CASE HISTORY

[NARRATOR: A fifty-year-old woman seats herself facing the doctor in his office.]

DOCTOR: What is your problem?

WOMAN: I'm not functioning well. I don't express myself adequately. I'm at a loss for words.

110

DOCTOR: How long have you felt this?

WOMAN: I was insecure even when I was younger. But it's worse now. I'm unhappy and I've lost confidence.

DOCTOR: When did you have it?

WOMAN: Some time ago. I had more confidence once.

DOCTOR: And when you had confidence?

WOMAN: I was able to express myself better.

DOCTOR: Are you married?

WOMAN: Yes. Three children, two boys and a girl. My husband is sales manager for an electrical concern.

DOCTOR: How do you relate to your husband?

WOMAN: He's easier-going than I. My temper is a problem. I say and do things on impulse, and later I feel guilty.

DOCTOR: Are you opinionated?

WOMAN: Yes.

DOCTOR: Do you like yourself?

WOMAN: No. I'm not very smart. And the people I work with are clever.

DOCTOR: Have you always felt inferior?

WOMAN: At times, but more so lately.

DOCTOR: What do you see when you look in the mirror?

WOMAN: A face I'm not terribly fond of.

DOCTOR: Do you have compassion for yourself?

WOMAN: I feel sorry for myself.

DOCTOR: Do you have self-respect?

WOMAN: I guess not.

DOCTOR: Do you hate yourself?

WOMAN: I suppose so.

DOCTOR: Why?

WOMAN: I should be smarter.

DOCTOR: When did you start disliking yourself?

WOMAN: Recently.

DOCTOR: Do you love your husband?

WOMAN: I did, but I lost confidence in him.

DOCTOR: Why?

WOMAN: He's too much like me. The inability to express himself plagues him too. But it bothers me, not him.

DOCTOR: Does he love you?

WOMAN: Yes.

DOCTOR: Why don't you love him?

WOMAN: I want to depend on him. I wish he was stronger— and more aggressive.

DOCTOR: In what way?

WOMAN: He's very quiet with me. Doesn't really assert himself.

DOCTOR: And you don't either.

WOMAN: He irritates me. He moves slowly on everything.

DOCTOR: Do you love someone else?

WOMAN: No. I wish I did.

DOCTOR: How would you like to resolve this problem?

WOMAN: Should I work to regain my confidence?

DOCTOR: Right.

WOMAN: How do I start?

DOCTOR: Do you have a job?

WOMAN: I'm a schoolteacher.

DOCTOR: It appears that you are stronger than your husband. Helping yourself may help him change. You must do something for yourself every day.

WOMAN: Like what?

DOCTOR: Happiness is a basic goal for every human being, regardless of age. Do you make the schoolchildren happy? If you're cheerful, the children will be too.

WOMAN: I guess I make them happy.

DOCTOR: You're friendly to them and to yourself? You are less critical of them and of yourself? You are successful with them and with yourself?

WOMAN: Yes.

DOCTOR: Then use the same technique for your family. Make yourself happy and the people in your family will be happy. Make believe they are your pupils too. As a matter of fact, they are.

WOMAN: But why don't they do something for me?

DOCTOR: It's your destiny to be the leader. If you make

your family happy, you'll make yourself happy. Try it. What have you got to lose?

WOMAN: I wish I could do it.

DOCTOR: You can, this very minute. By trying. I don't believe you really don't love your husband. You don't love yourself because you're stronger. Unlock your real personality and that of your husband by forgiving yourself and others—now. Stop criticizing others and yourself. If you make yourself happy and others happy like your school kids, you will find your self-respect. Insist on being self-reliant first. Feel too big to be threatened. You make mountains out of molehills. Just because you're a leader and your husband is not, stop resisting the good in you. Be kind to yourself and you'll be kind to those around you. Stop playing second fiddle to yourself.

[NARRATOR: Three months later a different person came to see the doctor. She treated family like schoolchildren, and found her true worth and the true worth of family. Through growing she became a happy human being.]

HOMEWORK

What does happiness mean to me?

Typical examples of happiness:

It is joyful to be vibrantly alive and involved.

Happiness means being myself. This is possible only when no thought of self intrudes.

I'm happy when I do not allow myself to be goaded into activities inconsistent with my wishes and ideals.

Happiness is a benign triangle—God, self, man, all in wholesome relationship.

Happiness means keeping simplicity in life and living it spontaneously.

Happiness involves the assumption that *today* is an extension of the holiday season.

Happiness means awareness and delight in little things.

Happiness is an extension of love.

Happiness involves reasonable goals and their achievement.

QUESTIONS AND ANSWERS

Q. What is a proper definition of happiness?

A. A state of mind characterized by pleasure.

Q. What is the nature of our functioning when our thoughts are pleasant?

A. Our senses are efficient and memory improves. Internal organs function better.

Q. What causes psychosomatic ills?

A. Unhappiness.

Q. The cure?

A. Happiness.

Q. Is happiness something we earn with good conduct?

A. It is not a moral issue, any more than is circulation of the blood.

Q. The concept that happiness stems from unselfishness leads to what conclusion?

A. Oddly, it leads to the conclusion that the more miserable we make ourselves, the greater our contentment will be. In other words, unhappiness leads to happiness.

Q. Is unhappiness worthwhile?

A. It perpetuates trouble, increasing the evil of the situation.

Q. When do we find happiness?

A. Now. Within us. It's internal. It is a mental attitude. If it is not experienced in the present, it is never experienced.

Q. How does one cultivate happiness?

A. By programming happy attitudes into the servomechanism, regardless of environment.

Q. What causes most unhappiness reactions?

A. Things don't go as we wish and we *interpret* this as a blow to our self-esteem.

Q. What is the effect of a lack of clear-cut objectives on our happiness?

A. We feel dissatisfied because we cannot tell whether we are succeeding or failing.

Q. What good is the happiness habit?

A. It frees us largely from the domination of external factors.

Q. How does one escalate unhappiness?

A. By adding self-pity and resentment to misfortune. We think in terms of panic and catastrophe. Aimless activity may also aggravate unhappiness.

Q. How are problems and goal-striving related to happiness?

A. They are essential.

Q. How do we color problems and goals?

A. In our thinking, we make them evil or good.

Q. How should one react to threats and problems?

A. Practice positive action, in both real and imaginary situations. Imagine confronting problems, not fleeing from them.

Q. Do we choose whether we shall be happy or unhappy?

A. "Facts" may lead to either pessimistic or optimistic outlook. We alone select our orientation. Disastrous thinking will lead to disaster.

Q. How do we program for pleasant thinking?

A. Resolve to remember pleasant incidents from the past; think of desirable elements in the present; foresee the future in terms of fulfillment.

Q. What is habit?

A. Habit is a garment worn by the personality.

Q. Why do we create certain habits?

A. *They fit us,* since they are consistent with our self-image.

Q. What differentiates habit and addiction?
A. Addiction is compulsive, with severe withdrawal symptoms. Habit involves reactions which we make automatically.
Q. Can one change a habit?
A. Yes. Make a conscious decision, then practice on the new response until it is ingrained.
Q. What leads to happiness?
A. Cultivating cheerful attitudes.

Acting more friendly to others.

Avoiding criticism of others and, when possible, giving credit for the good intentions of others.

Imagining that success is inevitable.

The Anatomy of Happiness

Now, what have you learned about the anatomy of happiness? To a degree, of course, this is individual, a selective process; but surely any reader must grasp the essential fact that happiness starts with you.

Still, how can you achieve this blessed state? By rising above misconceptions and artificial barriers and insisting on happiness as your birthright.

1. *Contentment is not a sin.* This should be obvious to everyone, but it is not. The masochistic person feels sinful when happy. The person oriented toward rigid "unselfishness" also squirms when experiencing pleasure. Remember, you do not injure others by being happy. It is more likely that, if you are unhappy, miserable, and resentful, you will affront the feelings of other people.

2. *Happiness is today.* Forget yesterday, do not delude yourself with fantasies of tomorrow. Live today, and experience happiness today. The present is what you live for. Meeting today's challenges, you chart your course to the mental attitudes that make up happiness.

3. *Happiness is a mental habit you must develop.* It is not a gift at Yuletide or a ray from outer space. *You*

give yourself contentment by building in yourself mental attitudes which will sustain you in times of stress, adversity, and catastrophe, even when others seem indifferent to your plight. You precondition yourself for happiness by winning your internal battle before engaging in the external struggle.

4. *Emancipate yourself from environmental factors.* This is not always totally possible. However, you can develop an inner strength that will hold up under the most adverse conditions.

5. *Orientations toward contentment.* There are such orientations, you know. You are considerably more than a puppet pulled this way and that by the powerful. The power is indeed within you, but you must will it strongly enough. You can overreact to misfortune or you can plow right through it with irresistible success impulses. True, you cannot control all environmental factors, but you *can* control your responses.

I will relate a couple of true stories that may be helpful if you feel you are stopped cold by "bad luck" or victimized by insurmountable handicaps.

You may, for example, be mumbling to yourself that Dr. Maltz doesn't know what it's all about. You may think I was born with a silver spoon in my mouth.

The unvarnished truth is that I was far from a member of the elite. I was born into a tough neighborhood on the Lower East Side of New York City. My parents struggled all their lives, and when I announced that I would become a doctor, people said this was not possible because my family lacked the funds for it. Later, I was informed with utter positiveness that I could not afford postgraduate courses in Europe and, still later, I was told that to hang out my shingle as a plastic surgeon in New York would be suicide. With a stubbornness born of determination, I stuck to my guns and achieved all these "impossible" goals. To buy medical books, I pawned my overcoat; to purchase corpses for my studies, I passed up lunch. It took time but I did reach my objectives.

This is not a boasting or a complaint, but fact. Certainly no tinge of complaint enters into this recital for in those days as a medical student, though poorly nourished, miserably clothed, and often uncomfortable, I was happy. I was working toward a goal for which my enthusiasm was unlimited; and hope filled my heart, sustaining my determination even when I was undergoing the most brutal hardships.

Now let me tell you about another "underprivileged" happiness-prone fellow, a fruit-and-vegetable peddler whose acquaintance I made many years ago during a brief visit to the Virgin Islands. He was lame, dragging his left foot. He trudged alongside his only real material possession: an oblong box of vegetables and fruits with inexpensive roller skates attached underneath in front and cheap wooden handles attached behind. This man was clad in simple khaki shirt and trousers, and he was a landmark of this primitive little Virgin Island community.

Every day he would come limping slowly down the main street of the city of St. Croix and every day was the same: vegetable and fruit cart, cheap khaki shirt and trousers.

Do you think I felt sorry for him? Not at all. He certainly lacked an expensive automobile and a rambling country estate. His clothes were shabby and he made little money plying his trade but, in truth, he was a wealthy man.

Why do I say he was wealthy?

Because his wealth greeted you the moment you saw him: his radiant smile, his cheery whistle, his friendly greeting, his courteous, sincere manner: these constituted his vast untaxable fortune.

His whistle was his trademark, and it trumpeted out a

message of contentment, a spirit of *joie de vivre* with no complications, a joy proof against disaster.

What did he have going for him? Just one thing, but it was enough. A happiness habit, unquenchable, indestructible, a part of his very being.

At fifty-five, this native of the Virgin Islands was not only cheerful but young. He had found life's most basic secret: the happiness habit, the happiness mechanism, the orientation toward contentment that requires no external aids.

Let us analyze, now, components of this happiness mechanism or habit.

1. You move toward contentment when you battle toward a goal for which you feel enthusiasm.

2. You find fulfillment when you achieve this objective.

3. The state of happiness itself should be one of your most fundamental goals.

4. Problems can and must coexist with happiness; no day is problem-free, but you can feel self-respect and aspiration while solving vexing problems.

5. Unhappiness is negative in that it makes you less than what you are; happiness is positive, increasing your stature as a human being and enabling you to make a worthwhile contribution to others.

6. Happiness and general self-esteem help you rise to your true potential as a human being, and, indeed, they produce more of the same: more happiness and self-esteem. This is a rolling-stone type of effect, a happiness mechanism.

A letter is apropos here. This one is from a young man in San Antonio, Texas.

Dear Dr. Maltz:

I'm sure you must receive thousands of letters like the one I am about to write.

I have been your friend and admirer now for close to two years. At a time when I was more depressed than I had ever been before in my life (to the point where I was even considering suicide) I wandered into a bookstore and, for some reason unknown to me at the time, picked up a copy of your wonderful book *Psycho-Cybernetics* (I seldom if ever read books when I was depressed).

I took home your book and found that the principles you used for happiness were very usable and needed in my own life. I was determined to try them and when I did the results were very wonderful.

I learned to make friends and talk with people (where before I was always tongue-tied and self-conscious) and also to make up my mind every day to accept myself and keep a positive attitude no matter what or how hard it was.

In short it was a turning point in my life and it was through the simple down-to-earth logic of your book that I was able to achieve this.

As I said, this was two years ago. In the interim I had gotten involved with other Eastern-based philosophies, falsely thinking that I had absorbed and mastered all of your principles.

But just a month ago I was compelled to stop and take stock of my life and to see how unhappy in many ways I had been the last year or so. Once again I went into a bookstore and once again you came to my rescue with the book *Psycho-Cybernetics and Self-Fulfillment*.

I must thank you again. The simple, to-the-point language you use helps me see in an instant the wrong attitudes and habits I had let myself fall into.

Of course my faults are still many and I'm trying to work on overcoming them, but now I can once again accept myself with compassion and be my own friend again, which is a very wonderful feeling.

I am twenty-one years old and I know that there is no "generation gap" in your books. The principles are applicable to men and women of all ages.

I know you are a very busy person and perhaps will not get a chance to read this but that's okay. I have gone two years now accepting your friendship and guidance through the vehicle of writing and I don't feel I can go another day without expressing my gratitude to you in some way.

Thank you, thank you, thank you!!! I don't know what else to say. You are a beautiful, self-sacrificing person and I deeply appreciate the help you have given me.

Maybe someday when you are experiencing a "down spell" you will come across this or a similar letter and it will lift you up in the same way reading a page from one of your books in the morning can uplift me and make me ready to face the day. God bless you, my wonderful friend. I am thankful for the help and comfort, for the guiding light your fine books have been for me. I'll say good-bye for now.

Sincerely,
Mike

GUIDELINES

To be happy . . .

1. You must stop hating yourself for every little fault.

2. You must decide between disbelief and belief.

3. You must have the courage to win out over a negative attitude.

4. You must use your imagination creatively, productively.

5. You must give; you must feel that you are needed. Remember the words of the Greek philosopher Epictetus: "What I made I lost; what I gave I have."

6. You must realize that the greatest miracle you can expect is acceptance of yourself.

7. You must seek the real truth about yourself, knowing that your most important goal in life is happiness.

Principles to Live By

1. Strengthen your self-image. Visualize the happy times and the pride you've felt in yourself.

2. Declare war on negative feelings. Don't let unrealistic worries eat away at you.

3. Get the happiness habit. Smile inside and make a warm feeling a part of you.

4. Learn how to laugh. Laughing, when it's genuine, is purifying.

5. Dig out your buried treasures. Don't let your talents and resources die inside of you; give them a chance to meet the test of life.

6. Help others. Help yourself. You will feel great when you give, without thought of profit.

7. Your greatest treasure is your self-respect.

8. Never retire from life no matter what your age. Continue to nourish your being with the emotional and spiritual feeling of contentment.

9. Seek activities that will make you happy.

10. Happiness is internal. You can find it now, today, this very minute. Remember the words of Horace: "Seize now and here the hour that is, nor trust some later day."

EXERCISE

In a serene, quiet room of your mind—in the restful playhouse of your mind—write on a sheet of paper or on the mirror the word "HAPPINESS," then read the following out loud:

"I shall each day honor the Happiness Principle, which in concise form means this: The more I share my contentment with other people, the more content I will feel. The happier you are, my brother, my sister, the happier I am too. Also, the wiser I am. Happiness is good; unhappiness is evil.

"When I feel content, the glory becomes visible in Nature. The flowers smell sweeter and the waters of the rippling brook are more dynamic. When I feel the soothing wash of contentment, food tastes delicious, the hand of friendship is firmer, and my voice vibrates with warmth and heartiness.

"On the other hand, when I immerse myself in misery, I can glimpse neither the beauty within nor that without, my ears seem coated in layers of wax, the flowers smell as if they were decaying, food is difficult to digest, my touch is heavy and listless, and my voice seems to retreat deep into an internal chasm, my soul is swallowed up in a wasteland.

"My happiness starts within *me*. It arises from my own clear perceptions, in which I envision exciting possibilities of growth. I refuse to shrink from these thrilling possibilities. In unhappiness, however, my vision is clouded by a mental cataract, my visibility is limited, fog holds me a blind prisoner, and I can see no good in me or in anyone.

"Loneliness, fear, paralysis of the will, senseless overlimitation, blind frustrated rage: these are enemies of happiness. I must overcome these negative feelings and rise to properly channeled constructive aspirations that will lead me toward fulfillment.

"I shall keep in mind the words of the late John Masefield, the famed poet laureate of Great Britain: 'The days that make us happy make us wise.'"

Thoughts to Live By

1. *Happiness is the one commodity in this world that multiplies by division*. It grows at such a rapid pace because when you extend the helping hand of companionship to others, they will generally reciprocate; and your own good feeling will accelerate.

2. *A smile is the launching pad of wisdom*. The wise

man understands that there is much complexity and tragedy in life. He learns to deal with it realistically, tolerantly. He also learns to rise above difficulty to constructive achievement and self-esteem through a growing sense of values that will grant him relief from suffering, enabling him to think clearly and positively.

Chapter 8

Self-Discovery: Your Key to Success

Does your mind live in a damp dreary basement, insulated from the world by impenetrable walls, screened away from the world by lethargy and terror? Is the door to your dungeon padlocked and latched and double- and triple-locked so that you can bemoan the emptiness of your self-imposed solitary confinement?

Unlock, my friend. Shape up to meet life halfway. Unlock the massive doors of your depressing prison, and move forward to success.

Your key? Self-discovery. It is through self-discovery that you unlock the invisible, self-confining walls that hide your personality, and become able to flee nightmare, escape stagnation, elude the shadow of inner death.

And now, turn to the playhouse of your mind, an open system, an integrated theater, an imaginative *tour de force*. Visualize the following illustrative dramatization.

CASE HISTORY

[NARRATOR: Raphael sits opposite the physician in his consultation room. He is twenty-nine. A year and a half earlier he was an unhappy man brooding about the future. Now a smile lights his face, which radiates happiness.]

RAPHAEL: One thing bothering me was what to do with my life.

125

DOCTOR: You loved mathematics and physics, I remember. Weren't you teaching young boys?

RAPHAEL: I gave that up. I decided to go into medicine.

DOCTOR: Where?

RAPHAEL: College of Physicians and Surgeons.

DOCTOR: That's my alma mater.

RAPHAEL: I begin this September.

DOCTOR: What made you decide on medicine?

RAPHAEL: My interest in people.

DOCTOR: You were so different a year and a half ago.

RAPHAEL: I've changed, thanks to you. I feel a responsibility for others. This evolved since I saw you last.

DOCTOR: That's *wonderful!*

RAPHAEL: Another thing I realized. Other people beside me are fragile inside.

DOCTOR: You used to think you were the only one!

RAPHAEL: I was not aware of others. You made me feel like part of the human race. I never felt that before.

DOCTOR: Fine.

RAPHAEL: I no longer expect miracles. I know what I can do. You helped me.

DOCTOR: No, you helped yourself. But you used to hate yourself.

RAPHAEL: True, but no more. I despised myself. I was intolerant of others and of myself.

DOCTOR: And when you looked in the mirror?

RAPHAEL: I saw a person with goodness and evil, capable of happiness and sorrow, of success and failure.

DOCTOR: Which predominated?

RAPHAEL: Sorrow and failure. Also, evil.

DOCTOR: What was the evil?

RAPHAEL: I was a shadow of myself. The evil was that I could not accomplish anything. I could not get my doctorate in school. I thought I had to be perfect. That was my weakness.

DOCTOR: You were resentful, too.

126

RAPHAEL: Very. I hated people who achieved. I was resentful because I was unrecognized.

DOCTOR: Did you recognize your own potential?

RAPHAEL: No, I saw only a shadow of myself and always sold myself short. When I visited you I thought that by using imagery I could restore the growth of my hair. But now the hair doesn't bother me. The *person* is the supremely important thing. I was not a person then. I wanted to be like everybody else—everybody except myself.

DOCTOR: Did you feel guilt?

RAPHAEL: Yes, I felt I wasn't like everybody else. But now I'm myself, a person, a human being, part of the human family. I share something with everyone who breathes and lives.

DOCTOR: You were terribly lonesome.

RAPHAEL: No longer.

DOCTOR: The last time you were here, did you feel self-respect?

RAPHAEL: I didn't answer you honestly then, not once. I was searching.

DOCTOR: And now?

RAPHAEL: Oh yes, I feel self-respect. I do not hate myself—or anyone else. I will not play that old record any more.

DOCTOR: How about your sense of understanding?

RAPHAEL: I understand my needs for the first time and the needs of others. That's why I want to study medicine.

DOCTOR: But you said you had no courage.

RAPHAEL: That was yesterday. You told me I had to believe in a goal, deeply. That I didn't have to walk around the world on my knees. Now I have a goal. I have courage, not only for myself but for others who might need me.

DOCTOR: Then you've learned to feel compassion.

RAPHAEL: When I learned to feel compassion for myself, to give myself a chance, I wanted to share that compassion with others. A doctor does that. You do, Doctor, don't you?

127

DOCTOR: I believe so.

RAPHAEL: You breathed that into me and now I want to give the breath of life to others.

DOCTOR: You didn't have confidence once.

RAPHAEL: I dealt with myself as a machine, not as a human being. Same with other people. I treated them as machines, not as people. Now they are my brothers and sisters. It's a surprising change.

DOCTOR: Right! And in a year and a half!

RAPHAEL: I wanted you to see it. I didn't know the meaning of happiness. I've learned. Happiness is something you work at, make a habit of, never taking it for granted.

DOCTOR: What about your feeling of insecurity?

RAPHAEL: I didn't know how insecure I was then.

DOCTOR: You felt inferior too, didn't you?

RAPHAEL: It was hidden inside me. After I talked to you, I struggled with myself to become a better person. I developed the desire to grow and see a different horizon. Now I see it.

DOCTOR: You were a shadow?

RAPHAEL: A shadow of emptiness. But now I feel wonderful. I was talking to an old friend and remarked how it was similar to the happy days of high school. I am enthused about life.

DOCTOR: Do you think you'll make a good doctor?

RAPHAEL: I will. Do you know, I feel like your son.

DOCTOR: And I feel like your father. So take your father's advice. Stick it out. As a premedical student I flunked organic chemistry, but stuck it out. I took the course during the summer and passed with flying colors.

RAPHAEL: I will. I don't doubt it. I have discovered qualities in myself that will not let me down.

HOMEWORK

What is the meaning of success?
Typical examples of success:

Keeping a well-balanced ego.

Living happiness.

Becoming a whole, wholesome person.

Doing my best every day.

Using past blunders as lessons for growth, not as sources of inferiority feelings.

Building optimistic attitudes.

Giving easily and receiving graciously.

Being myself and granting others the same right.

Recognizing that positive thinking is not enough; positive action counts too.

Accepting small successes and not brooding because of mistakes.

Formulating clear-cut goals and moving toward them.

Discovering my real self.

Developing an awareness of others.

QUESTIONS AND ANSWERS

Q. How do we recognize if we are success-type personalities?

A. We deal effectively with reality and gain satisfaction from attaining important goals.

Q. How do we build such a personality?

A. We shoot for realistic goals, developing a vivid picture of both the desired self-image and the final objective.

Q. The letters of "success" suggest what concepts?

A. S —sense of direction

U—understanding

C—courage

C—compassion

E—esteem

S —self-confidence

S —self-acceptance

Q. What danger arises after you achieve a crucial goal?
A. There is no place to go. You may lose momentum.
Q. What is essential after reaching a basic goal?
A. To pursue other goals or subgoals as soon as possible.
Q. When do you feel lost, purposeless?
A. If you have no worthwhile objectives.
Q. Why are goals so important?
A. Everyone is built to solve problems and to achieve goals. These characteristics give us a sense of direction.
Q. What ingredients comprise a sense of direction?
A. Aiming at a worthwhile goal, project or *cause;* working within your training or capabilities; maintaining a deep feeling for the present and for the future, not the past.

UNDERSTANDING

Q. What causes most failures in human relationships?
A. Misunderstanding and lack of real communication.
Q. Do other people respond as we do to circumstances?
A. We react not to reality but to our interpretation of reality.
Q. Is the other person wrong when he arrives at an opposite conclusion from the same facts?
A. He may be responding honestly to what he thinks is a valid interpretation of these facts.
Q. In attempting to reconcile clashes of opinion, what should we ask ourselves?
A. How does this seem to the other person? How does he feel about it? Why does he act as he does? Is *my own* interpretation correct?
Q. Can our *opinions* distort reality?
A. Yes. We can read malicious intent into innocent statements of others.

Q. What enables us to see the truth?
A. A willingness to admit error.
Q. When our understanding fails, then what?
A. Accept it as negative feedback, change course.

COURAGE

Q. If we build sense of direction, objectives, and understanding without effect, what is wrong?
A. We lack the courage to take action.
Q. Do our problems vanish when we ignore them?
A. They generally get worse. When problems are attacked boldly, they tend to lessen.
Q. Should one bet on himself?
A. Indeed one should. Research the problem, select a logical course, then move. Risk error, failure, humiliation. Once you are on an even keel, you can correct course.
Q. What if we don't build the courage to bet on ourselves?
A. It is easy to become addicted to gambling or alcohol or drugs, any destructive outlet.
Q. Do we need a crisis to show courage?
A. Daily living requires courage. By handling little things, we build the capacity to demonstrate courage in more crucial situations.

COMPASSION

Q. How do successful people relate to other people?
A. They like and respect them and attempt to meet their needs rather than to use them as pawns.
Q. Why does every person deserve respect?
A. Each is a unique creation of God.
Q. Supposing we do feel more compassionate toward others?
A. Then we feel more compassionate toward ourselves.
Q. With what are our guilt feelings usually associated?

131

A. With condemning others for their mistakes.
Q. If we grant others the right to worthiness, what does it do for our self-image?
A. It makes us feel more worthy of a strong self-image.
Q. Why do tyrants generally fail?
A. Because they refuse to recognize that people as people are uniquely important.

ESTEEM

Q. What is our deadliest pitfall?
A. Lack of self-esteem.
Q. Why is it so difficult to climb out of?
A. Because we create this trap for ourselves.
Q. How is this connected with *courage?*
A. We fear to bet on ourselves.
Q. Humility, in the sense of holding a low opinion of self—is this a virtue or a vice?
A. A vice. We must not look at ourselves as defeated, worthless, victims of injustice.
Q. Is jealousy related to esteem?
A. Yes. The person with self-esteem doesn't feel hostile; he doesn't have to prove anything; he doesn't fear losing love.
Q. How do we bolster self-esteem?
A. We must build a healthy self-image, stop wallowing in self-pity and begin appreciating our worth.

SELF-CONFIDENCE

Q. Upon what do we build confidence?
A. Upon past successes.
Q. Must these be major successes?
A. No. A minor success may be a steppingstone to greater ones.
Q. What technique do we employ with these successes?
A. Remember them, forget your failures.
Q. Does practice itself bolster self-confidence?

A. No. We can practice failures. Recalling successes and forgetting failures increases self-confidence.

Q. What bolsters self-confidence when tackling a new task?

A. Remember your feelings of former successes, even minor ones. Image successful moments. Remember that confidence is internal; you build it yourself.

SELF-ACCEPTANCE

Q. What causes self-misery and torture?

A. Using phony postures to convince other people you are what you are not.

Q. How do we avoid this discomfort?

A. By dropping the pretenses and becoming real.

Q. How do we do this?

A. Realizing the falseness of the old self-image, we must change the mental picture of ourselves.

Q. How does this alter the self?

A. We were born with the real self. People and things around us may distort that self.

Q. What does an improved self-image create?

A. It does not create; it releases powers latent within us.

Q. If not our basic self, what is our personality?

A. A focal point of the self used in relating to the world. It is the total of our habits, learned skills, and attitudes which we utilize to express ourselves.

Q. What is the meaning of self-acceptance?

A. Coming to terms with ourselves, as we are, with faults and weaknesses, but *also* with assets and strengths.

Q. Are these faults and weaknesses the real self?

A. They are acquired negative feedback which we have not used for correction. We are more than our faults and our weaknesses.

Q. What is the first step toward new strength?
A. A recognition that we have weaknesses and will always be imperfect.
Q. What bolsters self-acceptance?
A. Accepting ourselves as we are; recognizing shortcomings without self-hate; understanding that no one is perfect; seeing that biological urges don't make us merely animals; refusing to turn our back on our inherent potentialities.

A Voyage of Exploration: To the Land of Success

We continue our voyage of exploration, plotting the course, scanning the horizon, keeping track of the navigation. Our objective is self-discovery leading to success, and even in the age of jet travel and marvelous speed this trip involves no mileage at all. This voyage spans no huge distances and the energy crisis will cause us no concern; indeed, rationing is not even a factor to consider.

Our exploration involves an inner surveillance, a broadening awareness, a minesweeping operation upon the internal explosiveness, a defusing of potential destructiveness. Our aim, simply, is to get to know ourselves better and to grasp the basic components of success and to learn how they can work for us.

In our Questions and Answers, we spelled out the ingredients of the success mechanism. To illustrate more fully my meaning, let me relate another story.

On the island of San Miguel in the Azores, I operated on a young girl with a tumor over the upper left eyelid. The atmosphere was, of course, solemn during the proceedings, an anesthetist in attendance, another doctor and a nurse assisting, as I removed the tumor, saving the girl's eyesight and restoring her facial appearance.

A week after the operation, I removed the bandages from the little girl's face. The child opened and closed her eyes. It was a touching scene, for, studying herself in the mirror, the little girl wept with happiness: both eyelids and eyebrows were now the same. The parents did not attempt to suppress their tears of relief.

You will realize the point of my story if you will examine this operating-room drama to see how it can help you.

Initially, I focused on sense of direction: my goal was to remove the tumor and to give the little girl a chance to live fully. All of us must concentrate on our objectives, too: set goals daily and move toward them.

As a plastic surgeon, it goes without saying that I understood the nature of the medical problem before operating. You, also, must understand the nature of your life situations and your role in these situations. So many failures in human relationships derive from confusion and misunderstanding; we must all learn to avoid these pitfalls by driving to the essence of the reality. We cannot always anticipate the exact sequence of events. Even during this controlled situation, I could not foresee every eventuality and, as it turned out, I was forced to remove the tumor in a different fashion than expected. But I adjusted quickly to the changed situation. Comprehending intelligent adjustment to the need for new techniques and strategies is needed by all of us at one time or another.

I do not believe I have more courage than most people, but I am able to summon it up inside me when I need it. During this operation, I had to call upon this courage to enable me to accept the possibility that the medical procedure might fail.

Does this principle apply in a universal sense? Yes. We must all build the inner courage to take calculated risks, sensible gambles, and to proceed in spite of uncertainty. Everyday living requires substantial doses of courage. Daily, you must learn to remove the tumor of doubt inside you and to battle on toward your worthwhile objectives, choosing a course, and, if necessary, adjusting it to hazardous waters, unvisited before.

Most important, you must bolster your faith in yourself and not lose sight of your destination.

I had to feel compassion for this sweet little girl, and you too must develop a capacity for compassion. Feel compassion for yourself and for others, and this will provide comfort when the picture looks bleak.

Esteem, too, is important. Without belief in my ability I could never have performed this delicate operation. Without belief in yourself, you will fail in any endeavor before you start.

Truthfully, defeatism is your major enemy in life. If you cringe before the pitiful mental picture of yourself in your mind, you defeat yourself before you start. Work to build your feeling of self-esteem; make a daily habit of it. What could be more worth the time and effort, what could be more important to your future?

My hands were sure during the operation because the confidence of past successes was alive in my mind. I recalled successful operations from former days and this helped bolster my feeling that I could help this child in the present.

How does this apply to you? Recall your successes; forget your failures. Use the confidence of past successes to help you today. Feed your success mechanism with positive data, and it will feed you more positive accomplishment. This feeding cycle will reactivate your success mechanism and will help you to reaffirm true meaning in your life.

You must drop the mask; the masquerade is over. If you accept yourself, if you like yourself as you are, why do you need a mask? All right, there are ceremonial occasions and whatnot at which you may be required to control your feelings very carefully. But, what about the rest of your life? Surely, you have great periods of time in which you can drop the mask and be yourself, provided you can accept yourself.

What have I outlined here? S-U-C-C-E-S-S, as in the Questions and Answers. Discover the forces in yourself leading to success; it is a glorious exploration indeed.

Please read this story carefully.

While I was in the Azores, the Governor escorted me around the beautiful green island, a lovely place. High in the mountains were two adjoining lakes, one green and the other blue. The Governor related a fascinating legend about these lakes.

We continued then through fertile hills and fields of flowers and fruits. The countryside unveiled windmills and plump cattle grazing placidly. There were fields of tobacco and more displays of beautiful, fragrant-smelling flowers. Then, looking down from the mountain, we viewed an awe-inspiring valley of steam. The renowned Furnas geysers released great clouds of steam into the air, and again and again this steam erupted into the sweet atmosphere. The Governor commented that the people of San Miguel were fortunate to breathe such fine air and to have such fertile soil, attributing this good fortune to the purifying effect of the geysers.

This seemed far-fetched to me at first, but, later, thinking it over quietly, I grasped his point. It transcends the geographical to the emotional area. Just as these steaming geysers exerted such a purifying effect on the island of San Miguel, man could also let off steam and benefit. Yes, man also was an island and, overtense within the narrow confines of civilization, there was something he could learn from the geysers. By letting off steam, he could reduce the strain on the machinery of his God-given body and create a lush internal climate for growth.

Self-discovery? Yes, self-discovery leads to a dynamic reactivation of your success mechanism.

An insurance salesman mailed me the following success story:

Dear Dr. Maltz:

If I owe you nothing else, I feel the least I owe you is a letter telling you how you and your book *Psycho-Cybernetics* have both changed and influenced my life.

The very first time I heard you was at the Million Dollar Round Table meeting. Then I had the good sense to go out and buy your book.

Up to that point I was an average $1,000,000 producer with my company. When I became cognizant of some very basic principles that you outline in your book—more important, practiced these principles—the change in my production record was almost instantaneous. I immediately became a multimillion-dollar producer and the culmination came in this past year when I became the number two man in production for the entire country in my insurance company.

I hope and pray that God gives you good health and lots of years so that you can continue influencing the lives and careers of more people.

One of your grateful admirers.

Sincerely,
William R. Bartmon, C.L.U.

Another communication, from a man claiming that life "could also begin at seventy."

I came to America at the age of thirteen. I went through public school (P.S. 188) and through the East Side Evening High School. I studied architecture in Cooper Union at night, while I worked to help support a widowed mother. I soon lost interest in this field.

With $2,000 that I saved from my meager earnings, I started in the coat manufacturing business, a line I had worked in since my first job at the age of fifteen.

How could one expect to finance a manufacturing business, even fifty years ago, with a capital of $2,000? A cutter with $4,000 joined me to form a partnership, and even this sum was a drop in the ocean.

I got a very unusual break. In my second job, I had got acquainted with the sales manager of a fine woolen mill. This man was told by my bosses, who were very close to him, that I was okay in their book.

When this firm went out of business, I visited the selling office of this mill. I told my friend that I had gone into business with a partner. I told him I would like to buy some of his woolens. I was quick to add that we would pay cash as we had not issued a financial statement as yet. He said to me, "Knowing you, the statement you can issue, if you put it on soft paper, my firm will know what to do with it." He said, "We don't deal with cash customers. Everything we ship has to be charged on regular terms. If we are going to do business with you, it will be because I know you."

It has been said that for granting credit, credit men observed the 3 Cs, Cash, Capability, and Character, and I was sure lacking in the first C.

My friend at this mill asked what I would like to buy, if his firm would decide to sell to us. I selected four pieces of their best fabric at $6.75 per yard.

That afternoon $1,600 worth of goods, on regular terms, were delivered to our place of business, and I was told to sell coats. The mill would take care of my requirements. This was a pleasant surprise to my partner.

From then on the business kept going. We had some bad seasons and many good seasons. The coat business became a tough business, coming up each season with new styles, new fabrics, and changes of buying personnel in the stores, but I enjoyed it. It was a challenge. It was more stimulating than owning a plant, for example, that would punch out the same bottle caps every day.

In the past five or six years the demand for our product has fallen off, due to the mode of dressing. Added to this came the competition from imports from low-wage foreign countries.

As much as I loved the business, I was thinking of retiring. The decision was hard to make. Then came a push from a direction I did not expect.

The landlord of the building where our manufacturing plant was located, in Paterson, New Jersey, would not renew our lease, as this building was in the path of Interstate Highway 80, which was being constructed through the area. This news was a blessing in disguise. My thoughts of retiring were becoming clear. Who doesn't plan to retire? Here was my opportunity.

One evening I talked it over with my wife and she agreed that I retire and move down to Florida for a trial period of four months, and then for good. I looked forward to this trip. "At last, I'll leave this rat race behind and enjoy myself in the sun."

The first two weeks in Florida were great. Golf, the race track, and lounging on the beach. After two months I was getting restless.

One day I wandered into a bookstore and noticed a book with an odd title, *Psycho-Cybernetics, How to Get More Living out of Life* by Dr. Maxwell Maltz. I bought and read the book. In it is one passage that stuck in my mind, to the effect that the day is divided into three eight-hour parts. Eight hours for resting, eight hours for sleeping, and eight hours for work. The book also said you have to have a goal every day. What was my goal here? Nothing! But rest and sleep.

I realized what made me fidgety. I missed the eight hours of work. In addition, on my trips to the race track, I would pass older hotels in Miami Beach and see their patios filled with old men sitting, with their peaked caps, waiting for the Grim Reaper. In Tampa and Clearwater I'd see older people playing shuffleboard and resting while counting their days. I asked myself, is this what retirement means?

After four months I realized I'd have to have something better to do. I asked myself, what could I do best? The answer was what I had done for a lifetime. After observing the plight of retired people, I was not too anxious to join what looked like a colony of displaced persons, most of whom looked unhappy.

I talked it over with my acquaintances. They thought I was nuts. My wife was apprehensive; but she loves me, and agreed with me to go back North, back into business.

In spite of what I pointed out about imports and competition, I decided I'd cope with it like the hundreds of other manufacturers. This is a big country. There are enough stores whose customers appreciate the kind of quality that American manufacturers are able to put into their product.

Though I had quit for four months, I had no difficulty in starting over again. My decades of honorable dealings with my customers, my suppliers, my bank, and the union made it possible to open up where I left off. Even the telephone company cooperated and gave me back my old phone numbers.

Many of my old customers again placed orders with me with confidence that I'd deliver, which I did.

It is now the third year of my resumption of business. While I am not setting the world on fire, I am happy to have a goal each day. Getting home in the evening a little tired is such a pleasure, knowing that I have done something useful and come tomorrow I'll have a place to do it again.

Someone once wrote Life Begins at Forty. It could also Begin at Seventy.

GUIDELINES

1. Like confidence, success means self-discovery and improvement of your self-image.

2. S —See yourself improving every day.

3. U—Uproot the garbage of despair cluttering your mind.

4. C—Cooperate with your big self.

5. C—Convince yourself that you can be a winner.

6. E—Encourage the good in you.

7. S —Select goals within your limitations.

8. S —Secure tomorrow with self-belief today.

9. Add up 2 through 8 and what have you here? Success through a daily process of self-discovery.

Principles to Live By

1. Keep trying to see yourself as your big self, not your little self.

2. Build enthusiasm for your objectives.

3. Live creatively every day.

4. Resolve to understand the needs of others and of yourself.

5. Look for facts, not fantasy, and live on solid ground.

6. Encourage other people, and you will also give encouragement to yourself.

7. Seek to find your real self, your true personality.

8. Advance toward your realistic goals but, when you falter, have compassion for yourself.

EXERCISE

Your word for this chapter is "career." Write it down or see it in the playhouse of your mind.

Then say this to yourself:

"Each day I will devote time to the invaluable pursuit of self-assessment, looking to discover the best in myself and to build my big self. I will not despise myself for what I discover. No matter what my frailties may be, I will have compassion for myself, and I will seek to enhance the positive aspects of my nature. This process of self-discovery will be constructive and will encourage me to formulate fine goals, to move toward them, and to intensify my success feelings."

Thoughts to Live By

1. *Discover your capabilities, channel them, and move toward success.* Remember that psycho-cybernetics goes beyond positive thinking to positive doing.

2. *The individual who is truly successful helps others succeed.* There are not many successful hermits. Discover more than yourself; discover what others mean to you.

The Most Important Time of All

The days of Socrates and Plato? No! New England during the Transcendental period, the New England of Thoreau and Emerson and Alcott? No, no, no!! The most important time of all time is *now*.

Today is the time to focus your energies on the process of self-discovery which leads to success. Today! Don't be a "never" person; you were born to be a "now" person.

Chapter 9

The Conquest of Failure

We are all children of God, created with meaning and purpose. Obviously, we were born to succeed, not to fail.

Yet we are living in an age of morbid cynicism, in which Doubting Thomases often seem to predominate. Cultural patterns may induce meager expectations, impoverished aspirations, and attitudes tinged deeply by the deadly dye of pessimism.

This sense of almost predestined failure is a major obstacle. We must hurdle this barrier if we are to achieve any vital sense of fulfillment. It is no skirmish; it is a fierce battle! The quality of your life depends upon your determination to win a total victory over the dark forces inside you that would consign you to a status of second-class citizen.

Again, let us take off with another dramatization. Read it and see it—in the comfortable playhouse of your mind.

CASE HISTORY

[NARRATOR: A young woman sits opposite the doctor in the consultation room.]

WOMAN: I came because I found gentleness in your book.

DOCTOR: Thank you. But tell me something about yourself.

WOMAN: Well, my name is Alice, I'm twenty-nine years old.

DOCTOR: What is your problem?

ALICE: For the last six years, I have suffered terrible attacks

—shortness of breath, asthma. I'm told I can stop it but I just don't find the reason to stop it.

DOCTOR: Why?

ALICE: I don't know. At eleven my father died and later my aunt and uncle died. Suddenly, at seventeen, I was short of breath and feared I was dying.

DOCTOR: What is your occupation?

ALICE: Teacher for the last six years. I'm in childhood education, youngsters age three to seven.

DOCTOR: Do you like this work?

ALICE: I did for a while.

DOCTOR: What changed your attitude?

ALICE: My mind became obsessed again with fears of death.

DOCTOR: Is your mother alive?

ALICE: Yes. She also suffers fear of death. My father was violent in his illness. She was relieved when he died and feels guilty for this.

DOCTOR: When did you meet your husband?

ALICE: At eighteen.

DOCTOR: What does he do?

ALICE: He's a teacher at a psychiatric hospital, giving physical therapy to disturbed children.

DOCTOR: Have you any children?

ALICE: A little boy thirteen months old.

DOCTOR: Do you love your husband?

ALICE: Yes, as much as I ever loved anybody.

DOCTOR: What does that mean?

ALICE: I wonder if my feelings are genuine. I live an exterior existence. No one knows my inner feelings, just my analyst and my husband.

DOCTOR: What inner feelings?

ALICE: I am afraid to be by myself—especially in the outside world.

DOCTOR: Describe an attack.

ALICE: Well, I'll implant a feeling in my head that I'm afraid to be alone, that I am alone. I lose a sense of myself. Alice is gone.

DOCTOR: Gone where?

ALICE: I don't know, but it's as if I've disintegrated and at that moment the breathing attack invades me.

DOCTOR: Describe what happens.

ALICE: I take deep breaths, but I can't catch my breath. I get panicky and run any place to find someone to take care of me, though I've never asked anyone to take care of me.

DOCTOR: And how did you control this?

ALICE: By talking to somebody, getting my mind off the feeling that I'm short of breath.

DOCTOR: Does your husband know all this?

ALICE: I only tell him that I had a trying day.

DOCTOR: Does he love you?

ALICE: Yes.

DOCTOR: Do you love yourself?

ALICE: Yes.

DOCTOR: Do you respect yourself?

ALICE: In certain things like my ability to get a job done by being an excellent teacher.

DOCTOR: And are you an excellent housewife?

ALICE: Well, I could be if I wanted to, but I don't spend much time at it. I'm building what could be a profitable business for my family.

DOCTOR: How can you do that if you don't do anything for yourself?

ALICE: We're not successful at it.

DOCTOR: Whose fault is that?

ALICE: Our fault.

DOCTOR: You and your husband are at fault?

ALICE: Yes.

DOCTOR: How is it his fault?

ALICE: He's not working hard enough at sharing the business with others.

DOCTOR: What business?

ALICE: Selling soap products.

DOCTOR: How is it your fault?

ALICE: When things don't go right, I get negative and this affects him.

DOCTOR: Are you opinionated?

ALICE: Yes.

DOCTOR: What happens when you don't get your way?

ALICE: I fight back. My husband is easily dominated, very susceptible to me.

DOCTOR: Do you resent that?

ALICE: Yes.

DOCTOR: Do you ever forgive him?

ALICE: Yes, after I torture him by saying nasty things.

DOCTOR: He takes it?

ALICE: Yes. He never fights back.

DOCTOR: Why not?

ALICE: He's afraid to fight, I suppose, because he's not successful.

DOCTOR: Do you think you are a plastic surgeon?

ALICE: That's a strange question.

DOCTOR: Are you in the habit of molding people?

ALICE: Yes.

DOCTOR: Then you *are* a plastic surgeon of sorts?

ALICE: I guess so.

DOCTOR: You're a destructive one.

ALICE: I guess.

DOCTOR: First you must mold a better you, then you can mold a better someone else.

ALICE: I realize that.

DOCTOR: How about doing it?

ALICE: Where do I find the strength?

DOCTOR: From yourself. You don't like yourself because you don't get your way. And when you don't get your way, you get short of breath. What do you see when you look in the mirror?

ALICE: I'm afraid to look.

DOCTOR: But when you look what do you see?

147

ALICE: Me.

DOCTOR: Which you?

ALICE: Depends on the time of day.

DOCTOR: What does that mean?

ALICE: Sometimes I see someone I don't like. Sometimes I see someone frightened.

DOCTOR: How often do you see the little you?

ALICE: When I'm filled with anxieties.

DOCTOR: Write the word "FORGIVE" on the mirror in your bathroom. Look at yourself and say, "I must forgive myself for my mistakes. I can do a great job on myself by forgetting the past and living in the present." Have compassion for yourself and for your husband. If you are a true friend to yourself, you will stop being opinionated and will mold a better self not by demanding but by giving. For the time being, forget the soap business. First build the business of being a friend to yourself, your husband, your child. Mold the better you, the big you, the understanding you. Then you'll be a great plastic surgeon, a modern Michelangelo, chipping off the negative feelings within you. Your future doesn't lie in selling soap, your true security is inside you. Play ball with yourself, then with your husband. Forgive. When you don't forgive yourself you get upset and get short of breath.

[NARRATOR: Six months later Alice visits the doctor again. She looks happy. Her attacks of shortness of breath have almost disappeared, and she tells him of the new friendly relationship between her husband and herself.]

DOCTOR: And the soap business?

ALICE: We'll get to that later.

HOMEWORK

What is the meaning of failure?

Thoughts on failure:

To computer operators, "GIGO" stands for "Garbage

in: garbage out." If we insert the garbage of failure into our automatic mechanism, failure will emerge.

Failure can result from objectives that are too unrealistic.

Failure is "I should" overpowered by "I dare not."

We cripple ourselves when we weigh the known failures of the past against uncertain future success.

Imagination does not fail when it helps us to run, even if we cannot break a track record.

Our bitterness toward others indicates our lack of forgiveness toward ourselves.

We shortchange ourselves by magnifying failures.

Failure is not a lonesome road; we have much company.

Failure is regarding the rung of a ladder as a resting place.

Failure means inability to force ourselves to do what must be done.

Others' failures do not excuse our own.

Failure means constructing a haunted house in the brain.

Failure to find heaven on earth will not aid us in finding it elsewhere.

Failures are rarely accidents.

There is no failure when we extend the helping hand of love.

What we consider a failure another might consider a success.

Failure means standing still between two decisions.

QUESTIONS AND ANSWERS

Q. What are symptoms of failure?
A. F—Frustration
    A—Aggressiveness (misdirected)
    I —Insecurity
    L—Loneliness

U—Uncertainty
R—Resentment
E—Emptiness

Q. Originally, how did we acquire these symptoms?
A. Mistakenly, we adopted them to solve problems.
Q. What is the purpose of these symptoms?
A. To create an easy "life style."
Q. Why?
A. They are consistent with the outdated self-image. Any change would threaten that image.
Q. How can we change this?
A. By building a new self-image and recognizing that the outdated symptoms no longer apply.

FRUSTRATION

Q. What are two main causes of frustration?
A. An important goal cannot be achieved. A powerful desire is defeated.
Q. We all have frustrations which we tolerate. When do they generate symptoms?
A. When they involve excessive feelings of dissatisfaction and become chronic.
Q. What causes chronic frustration?
A. Unrealistic goals and/or poor self-image.
Q. Suppose our self-image is that of an unworthy, inferior person?
A. We will adopt this as our role.

AGGRESSIVENESS

Q. What causes misdirected aggressiveness?
A. Failure to utilize aggression in accomplishing worthwhile goals.
Q. What are symptoms of misdirected aggression?
A. Ulcers, high blood pressure, worry, excessive smoking, compulsive work habits. Also, irritability, rudeness, nagging, fault-finding.

Q. How can we utilize aggressiveness constructively?
A. Concentrate upon a proper goal within your training and capabilities.

Q. If you feel like snapping at someone, what can you do?
A. Ask yourself: Is the irritability brought on by my own frustration? What has frustrated me?

Q. What if others snap at you?
A. Perhaps I am not the real target.

Q. What are proper methods for eliminating pressures accumulated by frustration and misdirected aggression?
A. Physical exercises, especially hitting something. Write an angry letter, then tear it up. Work toward a worthwhile goal.

INSECURITY

Q. What causes feelings of insecurity?
A. Feelings of inadequacy.

Q. What causes feelings of inadequacy?
A. Measuring by unrealistic standards, ideals, absolutes. Also failure to maintain movement toward a worthwhile objective.

Q. How do insecurity feelings function as a "life style"?
A. They may constitute a built-in excuse for failure.

LONELINESS

Q. When does loneliness become symptomatic of failure?
A. When chronic.

Q. What causes chronic loneliness?
A. Alienation from the real self and from others.

Q. What causes such a sense of alienation?
A. Fear leading to shyness; fear of being hurt; feelings of unworthiness or, as overcompensation, feelings of superiority; unwillingness to make friends; lack of communication.

Q. Is loneliness utilized as a "way of life"?
A. Yes. As protection from involvement and psychic hurt.

UNCERTAINTY

Q. What causes uncertainty?
A. Fear of error.
Q. How does self-esteem relate to uncertainty?
A. The individual believes he should be perfect. Mistakes become life-or-death affairs to such a person.
Q. Is anybody always right?
A. No.
Q. How does self-esteem relate to uncertainty?
A. The individual fears loss of face if he makes a mistake. When self-esteem is low, he may feel that one blunder would be disastrous.
Q. How do successful people regard their mistakes?
A. As lessons.
Q. How is uncertainty used?
A. To postpone making a decision. If a scapegoat is handy, impulsive decisions can be made; if they fail, the scapegoat gets the blame.

RESENTMENT

Q. What causes resentment?
A. The feeling that we are shortchanged.
Q. How important is this attitude?
A. We use it to cover up everything—especially our inferior self-image.
Q. What results from feeling shortchanged?
A. Self-pity.
Q. What does resentment do to our freedom?
A. It turns over controls to other people and other situations.
Q. How can resentment become a life style?

A. We attempt to make failures more acceptable by rationalizing about injustice. We give ourselves the right to feel envy and hostility toward others. We derive the satisfaction of feeling like wronged martyrs.

Q. How does resentment clash with creative goal-striving?

A. In creative goal-striving, we act and set goals, assuming responsibility for success and happiness.

EMPTINESS

Q. What causes emptiness?

A. Lack of creativity and of heartfelt goals, or inability to work toward our goals.

Q. What statements are made by empty people?

A. Life has no purpose or meaning, there is nothing to do; how can one kill time?

Q. Can emptiness become a way of life?

A. Yes, it can become an excuse for not trying.

Q. How does emptiness apply to "success"?

A. We feel guilty and anxious when we have "succeeded" and still have no place to go, especially if our goals are phony.

Q. What are phony goals?

A. Goals important only as status symbols.

Q. Is there value in realizing our failure symptoms and negative thinking?

A. Yes, it can alert us to danger. We can take corrective action by substituting positive factors.

Plowing Through the Stormy Seas of Failure

To recapitulate, we must move through failure to success, rising above tensions and problems to meet challenges and to create opportunities for richer, fuller living.

Admittedly, this is no simple proposition. Life is indeed a stormy sea and, navigating yourself toward calm waters, you can be buffeted by fierce winds, rocked by swirling currents, chilled by frigid temperatures.

Many external forces seem to propel a person toward failure and frustration and toward the self-protective assumption of inevitable defeat.

This is why, to a great degree, success involves the capacity to plow singlemindedly through the stormy seas of failure, because this is a prelude to a countdown and launch toward cherished objectives. If you drown, you will not have another chance to restore your energies and to swim again.

Success and failure are conflicting forces within you. When war is declared, truces are temporary, cease-fires do not work. In the final analysis, you yourself must root out the seeds of failure before you are equipped to march confidently upon your objectives. The will to win, the will to lose; you must clearly see this struggle inside you so you can conquer the self-defeating tendencies and turn your potential into reality.

Salvador Dali, the great Spanish artist, once presented me with a masterpiece. His painting depicted a world half in shadow, half in sunlight. A midget trudged forlornly in the world of shadow, headed for defeat and misery, but in the world of sunlight the self-image of man was tall and stately, striding toward new frontiers of accomplishment.

Success and failure—forces that tug inside you. Let us examine the greatest enemy: the negative forces in you that threaten your self-destruction. If you can conquer these forces, you can win the battle of modern living and become a real true individual in an age when so many people are dehumanized.

Frustration. Suppose you drive your car down the main thoroughfare and stop at the corner because the traffic light is red. There is nothing unusual about this situation, but suppose the light remains red? You are immobilized in your car, helpless to move; and as the minutes tick away, the light remains maddeningly red and you sit grimly, waiting as the hours pass—and the light is still red. An outrageous fantasy, isn't it? Well, not exactly outrageous. In conjuring up this absurd possibility, I picture for you the horror of chronic frustration, a form of inner paralysis, in which you preordain defeat.

How can you overcome frustration? Don't set unrealistic goals, goals beyond your capacities. If you have already done so, reformulate them. Or, if the weakness of your self-image undermines you when you move toward your goals, the solution is to build a more positive image of yourself.

Aimlessness. This stems from frustration, and involves taking out your frustration destructively, negatively, upon people and things that just happen to be in your path.

The antidote? Accept defeats philosophically, regroup your forces, and channel your energy constructively toward new worthwhile goals.

Insecurity. Feeling inferior to others, naturally you feel insecure. Even when things proceed smoothly, you cannot shake this feeling that you are really a nobody.

Can you do something about this nagging self-doubt? Yes. You can understand that you are a unique individual with strengths as well as weaknesses, and you can try, try, try to fill your imagination with success images rather than failure images.

Loneliness. You feel not only separated from other people, but from yourself as well.

Solutions? Build a new, more tolerant image of yourself so that you can live with yourself harmoniously. If you like yourself, not only will you shed the feeling of loneliness internally, but you will never lack the company of others.

Uncertainty. You are incapable of making a decision and thus you take no action, milling around with the herd, refusing to assume responsibility for any initiative.

How do you deal with this? By understanding that no

human being is perfect, by accepting mistakes as part of living. If you can regard your mistakes as human and tolerable, you will be more decisive, because you will have the ability to support yourself during hard times.

Resentment. Chronic, unvarying resentment is a negation leading to failure. Of course, resentment is sometimes justifiable; but as a way of life, it can only antagonize other people and result in futility and destructiveness.

You can rise above resentment by practicing creative goal-striving. Set a daily goal. If you fail, try the next day. Another setback? All right, set a goal for the day after that. If you keep trying, you will succeed; and you will be able to rise above resentment to your full stature as a human being.

Emptiness. This debilitating quality comes from existing, not living. You feel that nothing is worthwhile, that life is a mess. It's just no use. Why bother?

The individual who feels this way is throwing away his most precious gift, the gift of life, more valuable than property or money or jewels or stocks and bonds. You must commit yourself to a relentless search for growth and enjoyment, struggling to feel more, do more. Reformulate goals for which you can feel enthusiasm; build your self-image so you can reach reasonable goals. Tear emptiness out of your bloodstream as you would, if you could, tear out a cancer—for it, too, is deadly.

F-A-I-L-U-R-E. Your worst enemy. No matter what your circumstances, you must conquer these internal negations first, and then move forward to more complete living.

You may reel under grave realistic problems, but you must not let them crush your spirit. Read this letter; I'm sure it will help you.

Dear Dr. Maltz:

I am sure you receive countless letters from people all over and I hope you will have a chance to read mine.

I don't know where to start but I must tell you that you saved my life and I'll always be grateful.

I am a housewife of thirty-two and have two children, a boy and a girl, and I live in the western part of Texas. I was happy with my lot and then suddenly I felt a lump in my breast. It turned out to be cancer and I underwent surgery and had the breast removed.

I made an uneventful recovery but many months after the operation, I fell into a fit of depression I couldn't get over. I couldn't get over the fact that I had no breast and that I looked terrible—and felt even worse, as if I were hiding my deformity from people, as if I were hiding some guilt from the world. My husband tried to comfort me but I had the crazy feeling that perhaps he didn't love me any more—that I had a pretty face and an ugly body. Suddenly I became invisible to myself—and then my husband gave me a copy of your book. I read it and reread it and found myself again. I came back to myself, as if I had just gotten back from some nightmare.

Your book gave me courage to stand up to this stress. I could find happiness in life doing something for my family and myself in the present—instead of feeling sorry for myself, I could live every day to the full and accomplish something worthwhile.

I decided to do something. I joined the staff of a cosmetic company. . . . I knew nothing about selling, but I was so thankful to God that I was alive, I instinctively wanted to help others, give confidence to others, the confidence I had to find for myself in those trying days. And do you know something? In three months' time I became the best saleswoman of the organization. I don't know if I'm selling cosmetics or confidence. Whatever it is I am happy and want to make others happy. Doctor, thanks for the book *Psycho-Cybernetics*. It's my bible.

A. Failure means an inadequate self-image.

    F—Fear brings about futility.

    A—Agitation, born of resentment, leads to elimination.

    I —Inadequacy makes you retreat from life.

    L—Leaving everything for tomorrow makes your score for today zero.

    U—Unconditional surrender of your self-image is destructive.

    R—Retreat to nothingness makes the climb to success twice as hard.

    E—Eviction of self is like total obliteration.

B. Turn failure into success.

    F—Fear is a human emotion; use it constructively to reach your goal; if you fail start over, with new courage.

    A—Agitation should be replaced with Atonement, then improvement.

    I —Inadequacy can be overcome if you set goals every day; move toward them with vigor, feel you are somebody.

    L—Leaving things for *"mañana"* is evasion; today is the day.

    U—Unconditional surrender of your self-image, never! Win a smashing victory over the termites of nothingness.

    R—Retreat may be arrested if you learn to cope with negative feelings and reactivate your success mechanism.

    E—Eviction is reversible; redeem yourself and return to your true sense of worth.

Principles to Live By

1. No one can make you feel inferior without your consent.

2. Live today, not yesterday.

3. Keep going in spite of your tensions, your pain, rejection, disappointment; never retreat from life.

4. Set a goal every day.

5. One creative thought, one goal at a time: road to fulfillment.

6. Greatness consists of trying to be great; stop short-changing yourself and start trying.

7. You are important; reactivate the functioning of your success mechanism and find your real self.

EXERCISE

Your word is "ACTION." Write it down, see it in your mind, mumble it to yourself, visualize each letter.

Here's a constructive dialogue you can hold with yourself:

"Where's the action? Right here; inside me. I achieve through creative thinking funneling into creative action. Have I always been a failure? Then I'll change. I'll work at an inner revolution every day—inside myself—until I change. I will set a creative goal daily and move toward it. If I fail, there is always another day to take constructive action toward another creative goal. Where's the action? Right here; inside me."

Thoughts to Live By

1. *Resentment cripples the person who feels it.* You might believe that your malice is wreaking revenge upon someone who wronged you, but the real victim of your resentment is you.

2. *Overcoming negative feelings is your first step toward self-fulfillment.* It is impossible to keep your eye on the shore of success while drowning in an ocean of failure.

Chapter 10

A Mental and Spiritual Face Lift

As a plastic surgeon, I have restored the facial features of many patients physically scarred by automobile accidents and other tragedies. This is not a unique operation. It is surely one of the more heartening aspects of twentieth-century life that an individual may recover from disastrous accidents to function again with a handsome face. He is renewed, reengaged, ready to move out once more with firm stride to confront the complex challenges of the world.

As time passed, however, I became increasingly familiar with the scarred psyches of people physically rehabilitated but mentally anesthetized. I realized that more subtle, invisible methods were needed to bring some human beings back to themselves. A mental and spiritual face lift was needed to overcome the inner destructiveness of emotional scarring. The batteries in the victim's psychological nature had to be recharged.

Take a look at an inner operation, a mental and spiritual face lift. It is another dramatization in the playhouse of our mind.

CASE HISTORY

[NARRATOR: Daniel, a tall handsome black man of twenty-five from Africa, faces the doctor in his consultation room.]
DOCTOR: What is your problem?
DANIEL: Well, I guess I don't think much of myself.

DOCTOR: Why not?

DANIEL: I lack character. I'm here because I read *Psycho-Cybernetics*. I need help.

DOCTOR: Do you have any family?

DANIEL: I was the only son. My father, who was polygamous, suddenly dropped out of sight. An uncle took me in hand.

DOCTOR: Was your uncle a man of character?

DANIEL: Yes.

DOCTOR: But *you* have no character?

DANIEL: I have sex with prostitutes.

DOCTOR: How did this start?

DANIEL: My uncle's servant initiated me when I was fourteen. I've been doing it since, but I hate myself for it.

DOCTOR: When you look in the mirror, what do you see?

DANIEL: My face.

DOCTOR: Of course, but what about your inner self?

DANIEL: Can it amount to anything? After all, I resort to prostitutes.

DOCTOR: Yet, you despise this habit?

DANIEL: Because it violates the instructions of God, as contained in the Bible.

DOCTOR: Why don't you stop?

DANIEL: It's too difficult. I escaped it for three months coming to this country. But, unemployed, frustrated, not thinking properly, I found myself entangled again.

DOCTOR: How often do you find a girl?

DANIEL: Nearly every week.

DOCTOR: Isn't it expensive?

DANIEL: Up to fifty dollars.

DOCTOR: And what are your earnings?

DANIEL: Oh, about seventy-five, maybe a hundred dollars a week. Actually, I'm unemployed right now, but I expect a job in Connecticut, in security.

DOCTOR: What is security?

DANIEL: As a guard in a building; it's part of a world trade complex.

DOCTOR: Do you respect yourself?

DANIEL: No.

DOCTOR: Would you like to build respect in yourself?

DANIEL: Yes.

DOCTOR: Do you feel compassion for yourself?

DANIEL: Well, I like to think I do a little bit.

DOCTOR: How much?

DANIEL: I throw away my money; how much can I feel for myself?

DOCTOR: Do you wish to be successful?

DANIEL: I want to be a successful man, a real successful man.

DOCTOR: What does that mean?

DANIEL: It means being successful in my Christian undertaking.

DOCTOR: Are you a friend to yourself?

DANIEL: Not really.

DOCTOR: You mean the habit, your visits with prostitutes?

DANIEL: Yes.

DOCTOR: Have you tried to reason with it?

DANIEL: Well, yes.

DOCTOR: How do you reason?

DANIEL: It is against my God; it offends my conscience.

DOCTOR: You could start today to change. Can you?

DANIEL: When the urge overpowers me, I read passages of the Bible to find my true worth. I pray to God.

DOCTOR: Visiting prostitutes is against God's will, isn't that what you truly believe?

DANIEL: Yes.

DOCTOR: And *your* will?

DANIEL: It violates my will.

DOCTOR: Do you recall the saying "God helps those who help themselves"?

DANIEL: Yes.

DOCTOR: How about living with that belief, then?

DANIEL: I feel I must do this.

DOCTOR: When?

DANIEL: Now.

DOCTOR: Do you mean this?

DANIEL: Of course.

DOCTOR: How can you begin?

DANIEL: By subduing my impulse.

DOCTOR: How?

DANIEL: By driving it out.

DOCTOR: You can't just say "by driving it out" and do it!

DANIEL: Why not?

DOCTOR: You can't drive out a negative impulse by willpower. You conquer it by substitution, by living in the present. You do something worthwhile and through that doing you find your self-respect. Self-respect is something you must work at. Which will it be? What is a worthwhile substitute for fornicating with a prostitute?

DANIEL: Maybe marriage?

DOCTOR: Maybe so to some people. But what else would satisfy your very own mind, body, and spirit?

DANIEL: Well, a feeling that would come from the heart.

DOCTOR: What would that be in your case?

DANIEL: Teaching the principles of God to needy people door to door.

DOCTOR: Fine, but when would you be able to start with this essential task?

DANIEL: When I am able to shake my personal problems.

DOCTOR: That is a delaying tactic. Here's a suggestion. Write on the mirror from above downward the word "SCREW." Say to yourself, "When I continue screwing prostitutes, I screw myself. It's tough to change, but I have enough self-respect to give my good self to a girl I can love." Now, it may take time to meet a girl you can feel this way about, but it will be worth it. Do you know any girls besides prostitutes?

DANIEL: Yes.

DOCTOR: Go out with them. Be a friend to them—with or without sex. Find the real friend in yourself. You don't have to marry; just develop a relationship. If it doesn't work with one, there are other girls. But get off the fence and try. Instead of searching for a whore, search for a nice girl. This religious feeling you talk about, live it.

DANIEL: It's hopeless with the life I've led the last eleven years.

DOCTOR: Your new life begins today. Forget yesterday; and remember that greatness consists in trying. By the way, your name is Daniel. Remember Daniel in the lion's den?

DANIEL: Yes. A den of trouble.

DOCTOR: You can escape. You are both the lion and Daniel. If you let it, the lion will devour your self-respect. The trouble is not the prostitute; the trouble is you.

DANIEL: That's the truth!

DOCTOR: You are Daniel the good and the lion is the evil, ready to devour you if you allow this. Who are you? The answer is within you.

DANIEL: How?

DOCTOR: Work on your self-respect and your compassion. Become too big to be threatened. Build self-reliance. Relax by forgiving yourself and you will forgive others. Since you are interested in religion, remember this: in the New Testament, there is the case of the adulterous woman given forgiveness by Jesus. But there was really nothing to forgive. Jesus asked the woman, "Hath no man condemned thee?" When she answered in the negative, he said, "Neither do I condemn thee. Go and sin no more." You see, Daniel, man lives in three worlds: the worlds of mind, spirit, and body. To fulfill himself, he must live creatively in these three worlds. Come back to your true worth. Make believe you are hearing the words of Jesus, "Neither do I condemn thee," and then say to yourself, "No longer will I condemn myself. I will go and (I hope) sin no more."

[NARRATOR: The next time Daniel was all smiles. He had met a girl in a school where he was studying business administration and they began dating. Through it, Daniel found his better self and was able to combine sex with love.]

What inner or outer scars bother you? Answer truthfully; it's the only way.

A few suggestions of situations that result in scars.

A marriage terminating in bitterly contested divorce blocks future contemplation of marriage, and even the possibility of romance is frightening.

Wild oats sown in youth tend to leave feelings of unworthiness.

Scars linger from a mother's invasion of an offspring's married life.

Misdeeds of people you love are branded into your soul.

Some scars stem from failure to act.

Insane jealousy creates fresh scars.

A scarred face can result in a scarred soul. The face is tolerable, a scarred soul unbearable.

Scars form when we resent and hurt others.

QUESTIONS AND ANSWERS

Q. What is the source of emotional scars?
A. Real or imagined injury.
Q. What results from scars?
A. A defensive attitude towards others.
Q. What is the result of this defensiveness?
A. It isolates us from others and from our true personality.
Q. Why do many young people seem to hate authority?
A. Injured by someone they trusted, they fear vulnerability to additional injury; they attack to drive away those who, if given a chance, might love them.
Q. What is the effect of emotional scars on self-image?
A. We regard ourselves as disliked in a hostile world.

Q. What is the impact of emotional scars on a good life?
A. They prevent it.
Q. What is the nature of the fulfilled individual?
A. He sees himself as likable, wanted, and capable; feels a sense of oneness with others; possesses a storehouse of information.
Q. Are we born fulfilled?
A. No. We must attain this state.
Q. What helps to keep us immune from emotional injuries?
A. Feeling too big to be threatened; having a confident, responsible attitude; relaxing away emotional hurts.
Q. How can one feel too big to be threatened?
A. By improving self-esteem. It is an active process, and involves formulation of daily goals.
Q. How can we improve self-respect?
A. By admitting ignorance and mistakes and profiting from them; by accepting ourselves; by feeling we have nothing to prove. With self-respect, we can't hate ourselves or others.
Q. How do we build self-reliant, responsible attitudes?
A. By loving, sharing, accepting, striving to understand others. Remember the words of the Greek philosopher Epictetus: "What I made, I lost; what I gave, I have."
Q. How do we "relax away" emotional injuries?
A. Reevaluate ideas.
Live dynamically. Every day is a new lifetime to be fulfilled—one goal at a time. Live in the present. Program yourself for pleasant thinking. Practice these nine concepts.
1. Be as cheerful as possible.
2. Try to be friendly to others.
3. Be less critical of others and of yourself.
4. Reactivate your success mechanism.
5. Don't harbor negative thoughts.

6. Smile once a day or more.
7. Readjust to each day.
8. Forget the pessimism of yesterday by formulating a goal for today.
9. Build self-respect, self-confidence, self-acceptance.

Q. What makes us feel hurt?

A. Our response determines our reaction, not the event itself. Tell yourself this: "No man is hurt except by himself." "Nobody can damage me except myself." "I suffer by my own volition."

Q. Why do we feel hurt?

A. By choice. We are not compelled to respond; we can relax free from injury.

Q. Why this choice?

A. Thoughts are things: we control thoughts. Every day we must yearn for improvement.

Q. How do we remove ancient emotional scars?

A. Forgive.
Stop holding grudges.
Forgive others *and* yourself.
Recognize that mistakes are negative feedback; avoid dwelling on past mistakes.
Remember that any inner scar is your hangup; forgiveness is your hang-on.

Q. What generates creative living?

A. Willingness to render oneself *somewhat* vulnerable. To trust, to love, to open up to emotional communication, means to risk injury. But this is necessary for creative living.

Q. What comprises the do-it-yourself kit for preventing and for getting rid of emotional scars?

A. Relaxation of tension to prevent scarring.
Forgiveness for elimination of outdated grievances.
A tough epidermis, but not an impenetrable shell.
Creative living, but with nostalgia for today and tomorrow instead of yesterday.

Cultivating the happiness habit.
The "geyser" principle, mentioned earlier.
A goal a day, every day.
That winning feeling.

Healing Your Emotional Scars

Now let us discuss the anatomy of the mental and spiritual healing process.

Are you disturbed by physical scars? Any competent plastic surgeon can work to restore your former features.

Mental and emotional scars are something else. These are deeper, often more painful; removing them is no easy task. The important thing to remember is this: it can be done.

1. *Your intrinsic toughness.* Basically, you are tough, and it is important for you to realize this. Most people have the capacity to come back off the floor, wipe their gloves clean, and, in spite of shaky legs, battle back after defeat.

Like the magnificent Helen Keller, totally deaf and blind, who rallied from her staggering handicaps to contribute so much to the world as writer and lecturer.

Like Walt Disney, who recovered from a nervous breakdown to assert his presence unmistakably in the film industry.

Like you? Why not? Find the positive forces in yourself, build them into a cohesive factor, develop a new faith in yourself that will enable you to rise above temporary setbacks and continue moving forward.

2. *Winning out over depression.* Of course, the depression will not instantly vanish. You may seethe with self-criticism, feel weighed down by guilt, your spirit may be trapped in a quicksand of self-hate.

The solution? Forget your grudges against others and against yourself. Substitute feelings and images of past successes to bolster your flagging spirit. Then, with your mood on the upbeat, set off toward new and inspiring goals.

3. *Your tonic: an inner belief in yourself.* See life as a game of football. As the quarterback, you should try to call the right plays so that you can roar down the field to a touchdown. There will be times when you will attempt to pass and the defense will burst through in anticipation. You, the quarterback, will be tackled and bruised.

A disaster? Not at all. A minor scratch; don't let it build into a permanent scar that costs you the game and future games.

Don't be accident-prone. When you are jolted, get back on your feet, accept the jolt as part of life, and regroup your offense for another touchdown drive.

Some days, everything will go wrong. You'll wake up late, the toast will be burned, and, after missing the bus by one giant step, you'll blunder into a succession of wrong numbers and short circuits.

Here's where you really need a tonic. What kind? Belief in yourself. This is the sustaining quality that will enable you to rise above irritation and frustration to that winning feeling.

4. *Forgiveness is the key.* If there is one feeling that can open your locked-up personality, giving it the invigorating sense of a mental and spiritual face lift, it is forgiveness.

Forgiveness is not easy. However, it represents your superhighway to recovery and reaffirmation. While holding a grudge may damage your body as well as your mind, forgiveness is the soothing salve that takes the sting from life's thorny moments and gives you the power to recuperate and rally. So, for the love of yourself and mankind, forgive—and forget.

5. *Resign from Grudge-Holders Anonymous.* It is not the kind of organization with which you may be profitably affiliated. Like Mañana Incorporated, it is an or-

ganization of substantial membership, squirming under the burden of too much negative thinking.

Like the proverbial elephant, members of Grudge-Holders Anonymous never forget. They hang on to grudges with the ardor of a miser stacking his money. Their blood does not flow peacefully through their circulatory systems. It is like sludge in a balky engine.

This pernicious habit binds the grudge-holders together in an association, but it separates them from themselves and from others like an unbridgeable chasm.

Heal your emotional scars; give your mind and your spirit a face lift and orient yourself toward richer, fuller living.

I feel that I can document my point most thoroughly by referring to experiences of ex-convicts, for if anyone needs an emotional face lift they do. So many former prisoners lapse into a permanent state of despair, unchanging, hopeless, paralyzed.

Psycho-cybernetics has been taught at the federal penitentiary at Leavenworth the past several years; hundreds have benefited from this instruction, fulfilling themselves as better human beings upon their return to society. Here is a letter from one who took the course and became successful after his release from prison.

Dear Dr. Maltz:

In preparing myself to reenter society as a productive and useful member, I have in these past four years given considerable thought along the lines of reestablishing my values and attitudes. Although I have learned a beneficial and worthwhile trade to support my family, there was still something lacking. Not being able to put my finger on it, I enlisted in various courses of self-help programs to try to fill that empty something within me.

I enrolled in a psycho-cybernetics class. As the weeks of instruction and study passed, I was pleasantly surprised that I had developed an inner peace within myself. Re-evaluating my self-image, through conscious practice of psycho-cybernetics exercises of a positive mental attitude, has filled my life. I am now prepared to return to society and my family, thanks to psycho-cybernetics.

Another letter from a former inmate of Leavenworth:

Just a short note to thank you for your recent visit with us at Leavenworth. It's not often that someone, especially of your stature, from the free world, comes here to let us know that, out there, there are still those willing and anxious to accept us and love us.

Then he proceeds to write of other things. I quote this ex-prisoner because his writing is gracious and tender. Surely anyone capable of such gratitude must have hope.

Psycho-Cybernetics

This Certifies That _____
has successfully completed ____ hours of Classroom Work in the study and practical application of the dynamic principles of
Psycho-Cybernetics
and in recognition thereof, be awarded this Certificate on this _____ day of _____ 19___

SUPERVISOR OF EDUCATION   ASS'T. SUPERVISOR OF EDUCATION

CLASS COORDINATOR   INSTRUCTOR   FOUNDER-AUTHOR

Let me quote another letter. The writer addressed it to a restaurant owner in Little Rock, Arkansas, and from there it was forwarded to me.

When I was in Little Rock the first part of this week, I noticed, on two occasions, the bulletin board message at your restaurant. It read: "Forgive others often—Yourself never!" Each time I questioned myself on the meaning, not of the first part, but the second. The message indicated that we should never forgive ourselves, and I do not agree with this.

Inasmuch as Our Lord Jesus Christ said that we should forgive our fellow man of his sins toward us, as many times as seventy times seven, we are, therefore, in agreement that we should forgive others often. However, the New Testament, in Matthew 6: 15, states that if you forgive others, then your Father in Heaven will forgive the wrongs you have done. Can we not forgive ourselves if Our Father can?

Secondly, Dr. Maltz, in his book *Psycho-Cybernetics*, states that true forgiveness comes only when we are able to see, and emotionally accept, that there is and was nothing for us to forgive. We should not have condemned or hated the other person in the first place. If there was no condemnation, there is no need for forgiveness. If we can truly forgive others, why is it not reasonable to say that we shouldn't condemn but forgive our mistakes? It is fatal, psychologically, if we don't. Therefore, may I suggest new copy for your board: "Forgive others always; forgive yourself as often."

A fascinating letter, for only through forgiveness can you turn your back on past frustrations and learn to conquer failure.

Why do I like these letters from ex-convicts? Because these were people who were able to rise above all their problems and frustrations to give themselves a mental and spiritual face lift. In spite of their overt antisocial past, notwithstanding years of incarceration, they were able to change.

But you who are free, are you really free? Or, self-destructively, do you build prison walls to bind you, so that you can hide behind your emotional scars? Then *you* are the prisoner? Give yourself a pardon, a reprieve. Leave the prison walls of your mind and spirit behind you so that you can enjoy creative living and new fulfillment.

Here is a letter from a correctional institution official in Florida:

Dear Dr. Maltz:

Fifteen inmates of the Avon Park Correctional Institution are pursuing a course of study in *Psycho-Cybernetics* based on your book. All have completed a course in W. Clement Stone's *Guides to Better Living* and are working through your book in seminar as a post-graduate study.

We believe that the concepts presented in psycho-cybernetics, when indicated, can result in a metamorphosis of the personality, enabling our inmates to return to normal society as positively motivated, functioning citizens. Results to date appear to be quite gratifying.

On Saturday, November 17th, from 4:30 to 7:30 P.M. the present classes in *Guides to Better Living* and *Psycho-Cybernetics* will graduate. We would most humbly invite you, and any guests you would care to bring, to join us for dinner and be the principal speaker at the graduation ceremonies. It would indeed be an honor to meet you, but would also be the icing on the cake for each of the members of the two classes to hear a "legend-in-his-own-time" speak in person.

It will truly be a memorable occasion if you can join us, and we hope that you will be able to.

This letter was signed by the instructor and, together with the material from Leavenworth, underlines the contribution of my theories to people who need to implement drastic change.

GUIDELINES

1. Fight with all your might to find your big self.
2. Build self-reliance every day.
3. Stop making mountains of molehills.
4. Pry open the clenched fist of tension and replace a frown with a smile.
5. Make your greatest life goal battling for self-respect.
6. Be a modern detective; track down the good in life.
7. Rise above negative thinking so you ean march eagerly toward improvement.

Principles to Live By

1. See yourself at your best, a person of confidence; not at your worst, a person of frustration.
2. Accept yourself as you are and try to improve, but do not aim at becoming someone else.
3. Practice forgiveness actively.
4. Exercise foresight, build visions of a creative day, realize that forgiveness applies to yesterday.
5. Stop looking backward to heartache; look forward to opportunity.
6. Develop creative insights into yourself and others; understanding means power.
7. Work on your sense of dignity. It is a full-time job.
8. Utilizing compassion creates a sounder basis of morality; use it to help yourself and to help others.
9. Set a prime daily goal of relaxation. Give yourself a mental and spiritual face lift, then relax.

EXERCISE

Your word is "SCAR" and, following the usual procedure, write it! Then deliver an insightful lecture to yourself:

"It is my responsibility to myself and the world to remove the inner scar afflicting me. I must negotiate with myself. This is a difficult negotiation because I am at war with myself, but I must declare a cease-fire. Insisting on my human rights, I must move toward my big self. I will create a proper climate, so that my total personality can flourish. I will eliminate my grievances toward myself. I will refuse to surrender to disillusion. I will see life's imperfections realistically, but I will strive always to seek ways and means for creative living in this imperfect world."

Thoughts to Live By

1. *To err is a human failing; to forgive is a human achievement.* Stop holding grudges.

2. *You are not free when you live with negative feelings.* On the contrary, you are more enslaved than the individual who has grave burdens and handles them with positive feelings.

Chapter 11

Unlocking Your Creative Personality

Too many people are overinhibited. Their feelings are double-locked and latched behind the surface personality they present to the world at large.

P. K. was like this. In his late twenties, he consulted me at my office, telling me about his stuttering problem and about his feelings of insecurity and despair.

I suggested that he read *Psycho-Cybernetics*. About a year later, he visited me again. The change was startling. He had stopped stuttering and, aside from this symptomatic detail, he was a new person.

This was of course rewarding to me, and I asked him to write in detail what had happened. The following is a profile which he submitted.

CASE HISTORY

Pre Psycho-Cyber. Personality and Outlook on Life

Before the changes brought about by the practice of [psycho]-cybernetics [personality] and learning theory, I felt sorry for myself and saw myself as a handicapped individual. (Others didn't see me in this light; indeed I masked the symptoms very well.) I believed that I was different from others, so different in fact that I couldn't possibly lead a productive happy life. I was obsessed with a fear of speech, which naturally carried over to heightened anxiety, withdrawal from people, and life in general. It had been emphasized throughout my life in school, through mass media, etc., that man is the only animal given the gift of speech. This is a prime reason for man's superiority over lower animals, and indeed it has often become the measure by which an individual man is judged. This became more wood on the fire for me to gain a perverse satisfaction at being handicapped in an area which others found so essential to success. I really believed I had good reason to be bitter, angered, and simply let whatever was going to occur in life happen. I was concerned that I would always be humiliated when dealing with people, and could never see myself as a success at anything. I therefore had to find ways of failing in any undertaking, thereby making the final outcome of any endeavor consistent with my self-image—that of an inadequate person who has a handicap which I attributed as the cause of failure, or which I kept sight of constantly. I could not see myself succeeding. In the final analysis I saw myself and classified myself as a stutterer period, and as someone that a dreadful thing was happening to, not as a human being with some good and bad qualities: stuttering is only one of these.

Post Psycho-Cyber

The first insights that occurred from simply a reading of the book without trying any exercises was that other people have problems of equal magnitude and are successful and happy. Even more important was the realization that what was occurring in terms of stuttering symptoms or failing, I was the cause of, not fate, or bad luck. I saw that because I anticipated stuttering or failing, I myself would find a way to fail. I was overjoyed to see that now I might be able to program myself to have successful experiences.

I was reluctant to do the imaging exercises outlined in the book because I did not trust the idea that the mind cannot tell the difference between a real experience and one vividly imagined, and because the method for bringing about behavior change seemed so ridiculously simple that

I believed it incorrect. What about Freudian theory, I asked myself, which in effect states that our behavior now is a function of past experiences? Since you can't change the past, you are doomed to be what you are unless you dredge up unconscious experiences and get emotional about them so they can't exert influence over you. This process usually takes several years and I was biased by a belief that any change can only be brought about over a long period. Freud, however, left out important variables that influence our behavior, namely the present and the future. Very important is the fact that I don't believe past experiences have any influence on present behavior whatever, unless they are in our consciousness now. I realized that I was compulsively dwelling upon negative aspects of my behavior and past failures (all conscious in any instances that I now tried to be successful). My mental imaging was constantly one of why didn't I do it this way, or you should have done or said this. There was a constant compulsion to dwell on the negative.

There was a sudden insight therefore that if I didn't consciously dwell on negative past experiences, the past is no longer here psychologically. Hence, there can be no influence. Physically the past is gone so why bother to keep it around psychologically? Physically we are new people every seven years, but only because we must wait for old cells to die to be replaced by new. Psychologically we don't have to wait. We can become new or reborn simply by killing negative beliefs immediately, consciously, by simply not dwelling upon them. I realized psychoanalysis deals with mental illnesses of the past. Psycho-cybernetics tries to keep your mind healthy in the present. I dispensed with my analyst.

Dr. Adler emphasized our behavior at any given moment as being a function of our future goals, and it becomes evident that this was my major problem. Whenever I would picture the final outcome or final goal I could never see myself attaining or finalizing the goal because of the speech problem. Therefore, my work toward goals seemed worthless, a waste of time. Hence, I had no motivation or drive to achieve (aside: stutterers on the whole exhibit a lower achievement motivation and not being able to picture oneself as successfully carrying out finalized goals is probably the cause). I realized that the start can be an incentive and the key had to be seeing myself performing successfully whether I stutter or not. You are either handicapped or not psychologically, no matter what your physical abilities are. If one sees himself as a stutterer, that's how he will perform. You must realize that stuttering is one fact of a complex individual. An article which was a good example of a person who used a handicap as an incentive was one which appeared in *The New York Times* a few weeks ago. The gist of the article ran as follows: a paraplegic became an engineer at N.Y.U., began designing crutches and other prosthetic devices, and now heads his own company. What the article emphasized was that his devices are excellent because the designer really had insight into the needs of the handicapped because he has experienced these needs himself. What I am saying is that this person saw where his greatest value to society was and indeed his handicap became an aid not a hindrance to success. This ties in with goals that are unattainable (it would have been foolish for this individual to try and become the world's greatest pole vaulter etc.). Many people have unrealistic goals simply because they don't know their own assets. Too many people believe the axiom "Be all you can be at all costs." I am certain that the costs to become all that you can be, in many cases, far outweigh the eventual gain, if any, and often lead to outright failure. This occurs in many cases because the person is motivated or prompted to achieve simply for the sake of achieving. That is, his goals are not his own; he is simply following the dictates of society. Too many people go to college simply because it is the thing to do. They are bound by culture and tradition. It all boils down to finding your niche in life, and you cannot possibly do this without knowing who you are first.

Who said if you stutter you can't accomplish? Who said if you stutter you will be unliked? Who said if you stutter you are inferior? I said it. Consequently I functioned "as if" these ridiculous statements were true. So my behavior was governed by my future goals but in a negative way. When I realized that I could be someone and productive with or without the problem of stuttering, there was a major personality change. I still wanted to do something about lessening the stuttering problem so I began to do some of the exercises outlined in *Psycho-Cybernetics*, predominantly the relaxation exercises to lessen tension and anxiety.

Then I began to work on specific problems, such as seeing myself move about freely and easily, speaking fluently, in such places as the college cafeteria, in asking questions during a lecture, etc. I found that using mental imagery gave me a strange or unique feeling because when you have the opportunity to try out your new self in the situation for which you have practiced mentally the experience seems analogous to a dream come true. You performed well in the dream (conscious positive mental imaging) and suddenly you are doing better in the real world. You have the feeling that you are in control of the situation rather than believing erroneously that the stimuli associated with a situation are controlling you in a negative way. The same stimuli that lead to maladapted behavior can be reconditioned to lead to adaptive behavior. I was not getting the results I wanted. This, combined with the fact that I didn't trust the idea that the mind cannot tell the difference between real experiences and those that are vividly imagined, prompted me to use the exercises outlined here. The rationale behind this is that by imaging only you are relying simply on internal stimuli and not using sense receptors from the outside world, i.e., eyes, ears, etc.; so there may really be a difference between vividly experiencing through the mind only, and reality. The point, however, is that if you believe there is no difference there literally will be no difference for you.

The problem was to make the practice sessions approximate real experiences as closely as possible, to gradually introduce increasing fear into the practice session, as an earlier stage of development and fear-producing stimuli was mastered (systematic desensitization). I set aside one hour daily when I could be alone and attacked the stuttering problem systematically in terms of reaching a point where I would be able to speak fluently in front of a class or in a classroom situation. Exercises in outline form:

Three 10-minute sessions of simply reaching about from a text, each session followed by a 5-minute break. Then, recording the number of errors made by playing back the tape, i.e., stammers, blockages, per 10-minute session. After about one month of practice, the average had dropped from thirty to eight errors per 10-minute session. What was more important was that there was a qualitative difference in the errors. This method of recording errors allows you to prove success to yourself; you can see for yourself the drop in errors. One of the keys was to practice in a calm relaxed manner so that fear could not develop. Another important point was not to concentrate on speech mechanism but on comprehension and relaxation. Once you have gotten about as good as you can with this exercise, you are ready to attack a problem higher up on the fear hierarchy. You may now want to prepare notes for a lecture. Go over the topic well academically, write your lecture in outline form, and then practice lecturing for a half hour or forty-five minutes daily. I didn't get good results until I began to feel and imagine vividly that I was in front of a classroom; i.e., imagined students sitting in rows (even set up chairs, etc.). I thought of someone asking questions during the lecture. You must make the experience as close to real as possible.

The next step is to bring a real person into the room and lecture. Choose a friend for he will be less feared. You can continue in this manner creatively, constructing exercises closer and closer to the final goal. Think success throughout the process until the final goal is reached, in this instance that of lecturing easily and fluently in front of a group.

This method uses many psycho-cybernetic principles, such as practicing in a relaxed manner, vividly imaging success, letting your success mechanism work automatically. It plays down willful or conscious effort of attacking problem, preventing failure, etc., but I believe it has advantages over simply imaging.

This is true because one can practice in a real situation and literally measure success mathematically. One of the great things here is that the success and self-confidence built up in these specific practice experiences will generalize and spill over to other areas. There is also a measurable satisfaction, worth, tranquillity, happiness, and pride gained in literally seeing the results of your efforts. In line with psycho-cybernetic ideology is the premise that we are breaking a maladapted habit and forming a new more adaptive one, that of communicating information.

Other knowledge and thoughts derived from psycho-cybernetics.

1. Life is a challenge and set up in terms of little challenges daily; you have to be able to handle pressure and tension. The only way to do this is by practice; practice at being successful. Therefore before retiring, I plan my next day's activities and outline what I want to accomplish the following day. By being successful each day and living in the present, you are successful throughout your existence.

2. It is not the actual behavior you are exhibiting that brings about happiness or despair but how you see yourself in the light of whatever behavior is occurring.

3. "Things just don't happen": Many people have the false belief that they have no control over their lives and go on

living passively and unhappily. If you want to improve in anything including the habit of living creatively, which includes a realization that you control your destiny, all it takes is practice, and a belief that man is a goal-striving creature.

4. By performing the exercises and gaining self confidence, a person can accept failure better if he does not perform well in a given area. The significant result is that it is no longer failure, because if you have a realistic and strong self-image, not meeting the standards or criteria set up by others is meaningless. You can still derive an edifying feeling, a feeling of contentment in knowing that you have done your best and are satisfied with your behavior in the situation.

5. In terms of job interview: What college should give a person is the ability to think creatively, self-confidence, and an understanding of one's strong and weak qualities and abilities. There simply shouldn't be an emphasis on or influx of facts per se. We know that we retain only about 10 percent of what we learn (by retain I mean being able to recall the information, whether the information is still encoded in the brain no one knows at this time). This combined with the fact that what is learned in college is usually different from what the graduate will be doing on the job, should make it evident that an employment interviewer is not so much looking for specific technical ability in a given area as he is looking for a successful person—someone with self-confidence. You have to learn how to perform well on the job anyway, so what interviewers are looking for is people who have a strong and realistic self-image.

6. The idea that you can do only one thing at a time has been very helpful. If work has accumulated, I simply tackle one problem and concentrate all efforts on what I am doing at the moment. The beauty here is that your success in accomplishing the first task usually carries over to the next.

7. The goal of any form of psychotherapy is to bring about a change in the patient's self-image, and it appears that psycho-cybernetics attacks the problem directly. Concerning my earlier statement, that the process seemed easy, it was not when I began to use the exercises outlined earlier. This negated my previous thinking that the process seemed too simple to really work.

Getting angry about my situation in life also helped. I knew I was gifted with talents but I was constantly met with frustrations. I persisted in my goal, however.

Finally when I stopped stuttering physically, I stopped stuttering emotionally and spiritually and I became a new person unlocking my real self, my better self, my creative self.

I have stopped criticizing myself and others. I relax. I smile every day. I compliment people for a deed well done, for a word well spoken, and I compliment myself for the same thing. I no longer say: "No! No! No!" I say: "Go! Go! Go!"

My goal? To get my Ph.D. in psychology and teach psychology. I love to stand before students and talk . . . and I can talk because I feel I have something to give to others . . . my successes . . . not my heartaches!

Thanks, Doctor. You showed me the way but I did it myself.

P——— K———

I feel fortunate indeed to have received such a splendid report from this fine young man; and, if I have not expressed this adequately so far, I am grateful to all the people who, in writing me, have contributed so much to this book.

Personality change is not a commonplace occurrence. More customary is the individual's inclination to play it safe, never to take a chance, to stumble through life in the same dull groove. This groove is monotonous, negative, but it provides a sense of security.

How much more exciting it is to aspire, to yearn for

growth, to meet challenges, to turn crises into creative opportunities.

HOMEWORK

What changes in personality have you implemented recently?

Thoughts on personality:

My loneliness is vanishing as I strive to make friends.

My true self expands as I shake off pernicious outdated habits.

As I come alive, I begin to resolve internal conflicts.

I feel freer and am no longer obsessed with dreams of freedom.

Dynamic, mobile, my personality is in no sense a recording; it changes from day to day.

My personality changes every day, improving as I adjust to altered circumstances.

Divorcing my former personality was like divorcing a shrewish wife.

QUESTIONS AND ANSWERS

Q. What is meant by a real personality?
A. A full expression of the true self.
Q. How is personality utilized?
A. As a focal point of the self. It represents the total of attitudes, habits, and skills with which we express ourselves.
Q. What constitutes an effective personality?
A. Appropriate dealings with the environment and securing basic goals.
Q. What differentiates the personality from the true self?
A. Each person is born with a true self. We later develop personality.
Q. What kind of individual reflects his true self in his personality?

A. An attractive person respected by others.

Q. What impact will this individual produce on us?

A. We will feel the basic quality of his personality, and this quality will appeal to us.

Q. How should we react to the individual whose personality is phony?

A. We tend to dislike such a person.

Q. What do we usually mean by a "good" personality?

A. A real expression of the self.

Q. What are symptoms of inhibition?

A. Timidity, self-consciousness, nervousness.

Q. What is the main cause of inhibition?

A. Too much negative feedback.

Q. What is the effect of too much negative feedback?

A. It makes us too careful.

Q. To what does too much carefulness lead?

A. Inhibition, anxiety, stuttering, and so on.

Q. What are examples of being too cautious?

A. Fear of saying something inadequate, trivial, or insincere.

Q. Why is self-consciousness really "others-consciousness"?

A. We adjust to social situations and others' reactions with creative feedback.

Q. How can we impress others?

A. DO NOT:
Try to force a good impression.
Act for effect.
Assess the other's judgment of us.
Lecture on some obscure subject.
DO:
Be yourself.
Relax.

Q. What is the difference between self-consciousness with others and self-consciousness with ourselves?

A. With too much negative feedback, we are self-conscious with others. Self-consciousness with ourselves means a growth-oriented process of self-analysis.

Q. What is the relation of conscience and personality?

A. Conscience is learned negative feedback directing the personality toward our assessment of right and wrong.

Q. What determines realistic behavior?

A. Clear judgments of right and wrong.

Q. Is "let our conscience be our guide" practical?

A. If our basic convictions are valid.

Q. From where does conscience come?

A. It springs from the culture. Psycho-cybernetically speaking, your self-image is your conscience. A good self-image means a good conscience, a poor self-image means a poor conscience. In such instance, you may say, "My conscience bothers me," which means you don't like yourself.

Q. How can parental attitudes toward self-expression affect the personality of offspring?

A. If parents feel that love, fear, anger, self-assertion are sinful, they can inhibit their offspring.

Q. What causes stage fright?

A. Fear of self-assertion or exhibitionism.

Q. What conduct shows a need for getting rid of inhibitions?

A. Shyness; fear of strange situations; overworry; nervous symptoms such as stuttering, facial tic, and insomnia; overcautiousness.

Q. What exercises could help to disinhibit?

A. Blurt something out, correcting it as you go.

Forget tomorrow and live today, practicing spontaneity.

Stop second-guessing yourself.

Raise the tone of your voice somewhat. This does not mean shouting; but a resonant voice may, in itself, be a disinhibiting factor.

If you like someone, tell him or her.

Personality: Escape from Confinement

"Personality" is not procured from the outer environment. It is released from within.

The baby epitomizes personality because, totally uninhibited, it does not hesitate to express itself. Cooing, sobbing, raging, smiling, the infant is superbly real. His state of freedom will be, for quite a period, untinged by civilized constraints or façades.

As we grow older and the socializing process begins to govern our conduct, we look for signals that limit our range of expression. A variety of obvious and subtle clues inform us whether we are earning social approval or censure. The trouble arises when we concern ourselves too much with the opinions of others. Then we become inhibited.

A well-known salesman-lecturer-author related that when he was away from home he was terribly self-conscious, particularly when dining in a hotel. He asked himself why; surely his knowledge of social etiquette was adequate. Eating at home had presented no problem. At home, however, he did not seek to generate a reaction from others.

The late educator-psychologist Dr. Albert Edward Wiggam was so self-conscious as a child that he found it painful to recite at school. Then, one day, he realized that he was not plagued by self-consciousness but by over-consciousness of others, fearing their opinion. He proceeded to build more self-consciousness by pretending he was alone, ignoring the possible reactions of others. Utilizing this technique, he became an expert public speaker.

"Conscience doth make cowards of us all," wrote William Shakespeare, and indeed conscience operates along the lines of an electronic computer. Answers provided by a computer are accurate only if accurate information is stored. Similarly, if your fundamental convictions are solid, conscience is an excellent guide in determining right and wrong. If, however, your core beliefs are not valid, your conscience may prove unsound.

Thus, self-expression may appear wrong to the conscience of an individual who was punished for showing off or self-assertion as a child. Moreover, a child who was punished for revealing fear or anger will feel that such emotions are wrong when he is an adult. This is in spite of the fact that, appropriately channeled, fear and anger may be proper reactions.

The child who was criticized for every opinion he uttered becomes an adult who accepts status as a nobody. Others, inhibited by a tyranny of conscience, take a back seat in all circumstances.

Are you one of millions who suffer from the pain of inhibition? If so, try disinhibition. Strive for less caution, less sense of responsibility, less conscientiousness.

Civilized society would crumble without inhibition. But we must differentiate between a minimal exercise of restraint to prevent utter destruction and overinhibition, which makes no real positive contribution while it causes individual suffering.

Thus, in a sense, we disagree with Shakespeare, for, psycho-cybernetically speaking, *we* make cowards of our conscience, since our self-image *is* our conscience.

The following signals or guidelines may direct you to a valuable middle ground between too little and too much inhibition.

If, habitually, you rush into things without thinking and your hasty actions hurl you from frying pan into fire; if you are unable to see that you're ever wrong; if you love to talk and brag and argue, you could probably benefit from a tempering dose of inhibition now and then.

On the other hand, if new experiences terrify you; if you worry constantly about calamities that rarely if ever happen; if you toss and turn, count sheep, and finally give up on sleep; if you always bow humbly to the will of others, you are probably overburdened by inhibition and would benefit from the following principles:

1. Stop rehearsing each statement you make unless it's really important. You're not a diplomat weighing each phrase before addressing the United Nations, and it is very unlikely that what you say, even if unwise, will trigger off World War III or bring on a nuclear holocaust. Chances are that if you blurt out something insensitive your spontaneity will produce no drastic repercussions. At worst, unless the occasion requires a supreme exercise of tact, or your blunder is stupendous, you may get a few dirty looks. You can endure these easier than you endure the stifling and submerging of your true personality.

2. Don't always plan each action in advance. Sometimes it will work better to act, adjusting your course in terms of developing circumstances.

3. Constructive criticism is fine, but stop destroying yourself with criticism. The overinhibited individual agonizes before speaking, then torments himself with what he has said. Introspection and self-analysis may be useful, but in too large doses it may prove self-defeating.

4. Try raising the volume of your voice, even a trifle. Don't shout or rage or scream. Just having the courage to raise your tone more assertively and aggressively can work as a powerful disinhibitor.

5. Remember that expressing positive feelings is heartening to other people. With good cause, you may suppress feelings like insecurity or jealousy or anger; but why hold in positive feelings toward others? When you like someone, tell him so. Chances are that the other person's appreciation will flow back to you. You might even break down and compliment your marriage partner. In these days of staggering divorce rates, this might cause raised eyebrows. Friend, do not let *someone else's* raised eyebrow crease *your* forehead.

Here is another letter, addressed to me:

It was a great source of pleasure as well as professionally gratifying to read your remarkable book on psycho-cybernetics, which caught and held my interest to the end and which promises reward on a pragmatic level far beyond the average. I am aware of how psychiatrists for the most part are chary of contributions to their field from regions of science outside their immediate echelon of knowledge, but the lively style and lucid articulation of ideas in your book must certainly disarm the a priori resistance of the most hardened psychiatric recluse, and arrest his thinking on the subject in a trice.

The fascinating utilization of Norbert Wiener's theories which you have so auspiciously put to work appeals to me as a solution on the therapeutic working level which promises great things. The clear and straightforward presentation of the dynamics as outlined by you is easy to grasp. In addition, any intelligent patient should be able to utilize the book either as a therapeutic instrument per se, or in conjunction with any self-oriented system of psychotherapy. I shall look forward to having many copies of the book close to hand for service in the aforesaid area.

Once again allow me to thank you for a rewarding and stimulating professional experience.

Sincerely yours,
Stephen H. Sherman, M.D.
Psychiatrist to the Blue Hills and
James McCook Hospitals
Hartford, Connecticut

GUIDELINES

1. As your own plastic surgeon, you build a healthier self-image.

2. You build this self-image from past successes.

3. Concentrate on the positives in life, and, regardless of age, you can alter your self-image.

4. Don't be impressed by what may appear as the perfection of others; they make their mistakes too.

5. Drop your mask, and allow your creative self to participate in your life.

6. Mistakes are part of living. Admit them, rise above them to the status you deserve as a professional human being.

7. Formulate your goals with enthusiasm, prepare for them. Get ready, get set, go!

8. Unlock your creative personality. V for Victory does not mean tomorrow. It means now.

Principles to Live By

1. Don't mull over each word when you have a goal in mind. Say it, then improvise.

2. Don't overthink. Cement your goal in your mind, then act, correcting as you go.

3. Let up on yourself. Exercise self-criticism more sparingly, using a dose of kindness.

4. Decisiveness means you are on your way.

5. Adjust daily to changing conditions.

6. Make enterprise, not emptiness, your habit.

7. Psycho-cybernetically, say to yourself, "Go!" not "No!"

8. Be a mind watcher. Hunt for your assets and for the reactivation of your success mechanism. Immerse yourself in the glow of past successes.

EXERCISE

On a sheet of paper or your mirror, write the word "unlock" and then give yourself sage counsel:

"To unlock my creative personality, I must reevaluate my internal assets and liabilities, engaging in an active, goal-oriented program of self-fulfillment, moving toward my big self.

"I will refuse to impersonate others, no matter how celebrated they are. I will strive for an instant me. How can I develop an instant me? Through days and weeks and months and years of effort, I will increase my emotional capacities and confidence until I have, at an instant's notice, instant me."

Thoughts to Live By

1. *Every day can be an inner revolution.* Bloodless, but revitalizing, you can bring about a dramatic rebirth of your creative self.

2. *The think chair is your launching pad.* From it you soar to creative adventure.

Chapter 12

Tranquilizers of the Spirit, Modern Style

In this modern age, technology reigns supreme. With cars and trucks barreling down our highways, jets thundering through our skies, and pedestrians running for cover, surely we have arrived in that long-awaited best of all possible worlds.

The trouble is that people do not seem to derive lasting nourishment from their material possessions. On the contrary, too many of us rush around like hunted animals, hands clenched with tension, muscles twitching, forehead lined with apprehension.

What we need is tranquilizers for the spirit to make life's pressures endurable. And that's what this chapter is all about.

CASE HISTORY

[NARRATOR: The woman sitting opposite the doctor in the consultation room appears agitated.]

DOCTOR: What is your name?

WOMAN: Louise.

DOCTOR: Age?

LOUISE: Fifty.

DOCTOR: Occupation?

LOUISE: I'm a housewife.

DOCTOR: Any sideline?

LOUISE: Yes. I do sculpture.

DOCTOR: Are you good at it?

LOUISE: Fairly.

DOCTOR: What is your problem?

LOUISE: Oh, I'm nervous. I jump at noises, like the ringing of the telephone. Thunder and lightning scare me half to death.

DOCTOR: When did this start?

LOUISE: When I was about twelve. I was in Belgium during wartime; the bombing terrified me. Later, I left for South America.

DOCTOR: How long were you there?

LOUISE: I was in Lima, Peru, for seventeen years.

DOCTOR: When did you come to the United States?

LOUISE: Two years ago. But, like the bombing, lightning still frightens me. So does the telephone. And I can't eat. I have spasms in my stomach.

DOCTOR: When did you begin sculpturing?

LOUISE: Twelve years ago, in Peru.

DOCTOR: Are you married?

LOUISE: Yes. Seventeen years.

DOCTOR: Tell me about your husband?

LOUISE: He's an engineer in textiles.

DOCTOR: Do you have any children?

LOUISE: Yes, three.

DOCTOR: Are they afraid of thunder and lightning and the ringing of the telephone?

LOUISE: No.

DOCTOR: Do you get along with your husband?

LOUISE: Yes. He was born in Poland but lived for a while in Peru.

DOCTOR: When you look in the mirror, what do you see?

LOUISE: Myself.

DOCTOR: Is that your real self?

LOUISE: I don't really know.

DOCTOR: Who would you like to be?

LOUISE: I wouldn't like to be anybody else, if that's what you mean. Just my strong self.

DOCTOR: What's stopping you then?

LOUISE: My constitution.

DOCTOR: Do you believe that? I don't.

LOUISE: When I hear noise, like the ringing of the telephone, I shake.

DOCTOR: Were any of your family members killed during the bombing of Belgium?

LOUISE: No.

DOCTOR: Do you respect yourself?

LOUISE: Yes, more or less.

DOCTOR: Do you believe in yourself?

LOUISE: I guess.

DOCTOR: How much do you live in the present?

LOUISE: Off and on.

DOCTOR: I believe you live too much in the past. Take the noises that bother you so much. Doesn't the ringing of the telephone take you back deep into yesterday?

LOUISE: I recall my mother's illness.

DOCTOR: Oh?

LOUISE: In Belgium during the war, in Brussels.

DOCTOR: You must forget yesterday.

LOUISE: I wish I could.

DOCTOR: Now is your key. You must live now.

LOUISE: I'm ashamed to complain because I wasn't even in a concentration camp; but I can't help it.

DOCTOR: Do you love your husband?

LOUISE: Very much.

DOCTOR: What about your children? Do you love them?

LOUISE: Oh, yes!

DOCTOR: But, do you love *yourself*?

LOUISE: I don't know.

DOCTOR: When do you wish to live—today or yesterday?

LOUISE: Today, believe me; but show me how?

DOCTOR: What did you say about your mother?

LOUISE: She was ill. Then the telephone started ringing, and the Nazis came. She was taken to the hospital, but I escaped. I never saw her again.

DOCTOR: I understand how you feel. But you must forget this tragedy and live in the present with your family. Look, you're a sculptor. Let me tell you a story about the great Michelangelo. As a young man, he saw a huge block of stone in a quarry and said to himself, "I see Moses there," and with hammer and chisel he chipped away at the marble. After many many months of dedicated labor, there was Moses.

LOUISE: But I'm not Michelangelo.

DOCTOR: Of course not. But you are a sculptor in your own right, and you must become another kind of sculptor— reshaping your mind, psychologically chipping away the hurts and fears of yesterday. Tell me, what kind of sculpture do you do?

LOUISE: Abstract.

DOCTOR: Do something concrete; mold something out of yourself.

LOUISE: How?

DOCTOR: I will tell you another story first. It's about a middle-aged woman who, many years ago, escaped the Nazi terror in Germany. Her husband and children were murdered in a concentration camp. She herself had tattooed numbers on her left arm. For many years a displaced person, she was terribly depressed and on several occasions felt like committing suicide. She found it impossible to lose the horror of the past. Then she met a man, they fell in love, and she was finally able to shake the miseries of yesterday and live in the present.

LOUISE: She must have gone through hell.

DOCTOR: Yes, but she decided to let go of her death in the past in favor of life in the present. All of us must suffer through periods of grief, but we must learn to rise above these times of pain and horror, not allowing grief to become our life. And this woman made up her mind that no longer would she accept status as a displaced person. Instead, she decided to build a new life.

LOUISE: Good for her.

DOCTOR: Sure, but what about you?

LOUISE: Well, where do I begin?

DOCTOR: You escaped the concentration camp, you say. Have you really escaped?

LOUISE: What do you mean?

DOCTOR: Since the Nazis came for your mother, you've been in a concentration camp. Your heartaches, your fears: they have created a concentration camp inside you. You've retreated into the dark tunnels of your troubled mind. You have built this hell for yourself. Since the day you escaped this hideous fate, you have made yourself a displaced person.

LOUISE: Yes, that's true.

DOCTOR: Try this exercise every time you have a chance. Go over to your bathroom mirror and write the word "ME" on it in lipstick. Then, when you look in the mirror, say to yourself, "Who am I? Am I the little me of yesterday or the big me of today? You see, Louise, millions of people who have never seen a concentration camp build a mental one inside their mind through misfortune, heartache, error, resentment, or fear. They are displaced persons, for every day they displace themselves from goodness and hope to inner despair. Yet, with compassion, they could remove the barbed wire circling their spiritual concentration camp, emerging from their dungeon into the dawn of a new productive day. Do you understand my message?

LOUISE: Yes.

DOCTOR: Years ago a blackout enveloped the eastern part of the United States and Canada. Thirty million people or thereabouts were trapped in this blackout, which was beyond their control. But you, Louise, and many millions create their own blackout, a mental and spiritual form of blackout, and this is an inestimably more severe condition. You must emerge from this state, demonstrating your self-respect as a human being, striding out of this blackout and returning in triumph to your true self.

LOUISE: It won't be easy.

DOCTOR: Granted, it won't be easy, but it *is* necessary. Too many of us build mental prison walls around ourselves and these walls surround us every day of our lives. Tear down these prison walls and regain your freedom. Remember this: No one can make you a displaced person without your consent and no one can imprison you without your consent.

LOUISE: Yes, but——

DOCTOR: Here's another suggestion. After about a month, remove the word "ME" from your mirror and write down "NUMBER ONE" instead. Leave it there a while and, studying it, say to yourself, "With pride, I will rise above the tensions and stresses of yesterday to find my big self today. From now on, I am number one. . . . Maybe not to the world, but I will be number one to myself and my family."

LOUISE: I'll give it a try.

DOCTOR: Every day, take a little vacation for five minutes. Sit in a quiet room or in a room in the playhouse of your mind. Relax, opening your tight fists to make visible the palms of your hands. Turn a frown into a smile. Pretend you are walking out of a decompression chamber, leaving the feeling of inadequacy behind you. Look outside the window of your mind to a lovely green garden, in which the sun shines brightly. In the distance a geyser is letting off steam. This should be a symbol for you to let go of your tensions for a moment, breaking the electric circuit of distress, renewing your energies for a creative day ahead. I've learned to do this and so have many others. Will you try?

LOUISE: I will.

DOCTOR: And, if the telephone rings, delay answering it and let it ring, a reminder that you are living today, not yesterday; say to yourself, "I'll answer the phone later."

LOUISE: I hope it will work.

DOCTOR: I assure you it will. I recall when I performed surgery in the hot Central American countries that women in the midday sun would carry black umbrellas to protect themselves from sunstroke. When the telephone rings, make believe you are wearing a psychic umbrella to shield you from a tension stroke. Delay your response.

LOUISE: Okay.

[NARRATOR: About eight months later, Louise paid another visit to the doctor. She had made a sharp adjustment, moving toward her better self, living in the present. She had found peace of mind without taking tranquilizing pills. When the telephone rings, she lets it ring for a while, remembering that it is time to relax. Then, after a while, she picks up the phone.]

HOMEWORK

Furnish your quiet room.

Thoughts on the quiet room:

An austere room, with single chair and a splendid view from the window. You reach the room by climbing carpeted stairs, depositing a worry or problem on each step, symbolically, as you climb. You enter the room and shut out all sound by closing the door.

You sit under a coconut tree on a glistening white beach and are at peace.

Your living room is partitioned off, allowing you to find seclusion in the midst of noise.

You sit in a plush room, with many chairs, a grand piano, plush carpeting, French windows opening onto a formal lawn; reclining on a chaise longue, you savor the comfort but you focus on the contentment in your mind, not on the extravagance of the furnishings.

A rustic porch of a country house on a mountainside. Here you recline, inhaling the pure air, in a rocking chair. Your thoughts are as serene as your surroundings.

Q. What is the effect of tranquilizers?

A. They minimize our reaction to troublesome factors. We do not overreact.

Q. What is the effect of tranquilizers on negative feedback?

A. They tone down the reaction to such feedback.

Q. How can we reduce overreaction to negative feedback without the use of tranquilizers?

A. Let the telephone ring; delay answering it. Stop being imperative.

Q. Are we conditioned to react to the ringing of the telephone and so forth?

A. Yes, we have many buttons for triggered responses.

Q. Are these responses free?

A. No. We react like puppets.

Q. What about conditioned reactions to fear?

A. They are built in.

Q. Any other suggestion (besides letting the phone ring) for curbing overreaction?

A. Relax.

Q. What will help us let the phone ring?

A. Seeing ourselves sitting relaxed, not responding.

Q. What if the response is too strong to ignore?

A. Delay it.

Q. What is the effect of delay on conditioned responses?

A. It breaks up the pattern, providing time for arriving at a proper response.

Q. What is behind hostility, insecurity, fear?

A. Our internal reaction, not the external situation.

Q. What happens when we allow ourselves to respond?

A. Tension results.

Q. When we are relaxed, what is the effect on hostility, insecurity, fear?

A. They vanish.

Q. Why is this?

A. Relaxation of muscles aids relaxation of the mind.

Q. What is nature's tranquilizer?

A. Relaxation.

Q. What is the purpose of a quiet room in our mind?

A. We need a brief daily escape from problems.

Q. What are insomnia and rudeness the result of?

A. An emotional hangover from frustration, worry, and so on.

Q. Can emotional hangovers cause accidents?

A. Yes.

Q. Can fear and anger affect driving skill?

A. Yes. Fear and anger cause tension and tension is a negative factor in terms of driving.

Q. How do such feelings as love, friendliness, and so on, affect tranquillity?

A. Positively, reducing tension.

Q. Is there a clue here regarding use of the quiet room?

A. Yes. Accept these soothing feelings.

Q. What determines your state of mind?

A. Not external forces, but your reaction to them.

Q. Suppose you do not react?

A. Then you will not feel irritated.

Q. In what fashion does our nervous system respond to imaginary emotional problems?

A. The nervous system cannot differentiate between real and imaginary.

Q. What is an appropriate reaction to worrisome images?

A. Overlook them. Live emotionally today and you will have no time to react to imaginary worries.

Q. Are there two possible uses of the quiet room?

A. Yes. As a daily tranquilizer, and to shake yourself clear of "carried-over" emotions.

Q. What exercises will be conducive to tranquillity?

A. Practice nonreacting to upsetting situations. Let the telephone ring.
Q. What may follow from building a mental and spiritual thermostat?
A. We can escape externals.

Keys to Tolerance of Stress

Toward the end of World War II, Harry S. Truman, then President, was asked how he was able to keep his cool under the pressures of his office. He said that he had a "foxhole" in his mind and that just as, in combat, the infantryman could scramble into his foxhole to take cover, he relied on a "mental foxhole" in times of stress.

The philosopher Marcus Aurelius shared this conviction. He believed devoutly that a human being needed the capacity to retreat within himself to acquire peace of mind and inner renewal.

In a sense, this explains the recent popularity of tranquilizer pills, which screen us from disturbing forces in the environment. What they change is not the actual environment, but one's reaction to these forces.

Our feelings of disturbance stem from our reactions, not from externals in the environment. Therefore, by monitoring these reactions, we build our own psychic screen. Reaction involves tension; at the opposite pole to this is relaxation.

As an example, let us assume that your telephone commences to ring and, automatically, unthinkingly, you rush to respond to its strident summons. But why the urgency of your reaction? Instead, why could you not relax by ignoring it?

Utilize this principle in other contexts to overcome this type of conditioned reaction. Again, in different circumstances, evade the side effects of stress by "letting the telephone ring."

If total nonreaction is not possible, delay your response. Delay may curb an automatic response totally and in any case may allow you to cope more effectively with the tension-arousing stimulus.

After learning the basic secret of tranquillity, overcoming a conditioned move to tension, we may discover within us a quiet room in which we can find serenity. Build such a room in your imagination, a ready-made retreat in which you may find peace during periods of tension.

Then, when the world becomes too much, retire into this quiet room in your mind. Here you may draw upon your inner resources so that you can weather crises. You will be able to invest in your ability to renew yourself when you need it most.

Mental images can serve a useful purpose. As an example, I have often used the image of a geyser erupting to help myself rally from hypertense periods. Retiring into my serene mental room, in a symbolic sense I would erupt, imagining waves of emotional steam exploding from my head to evaporate in the air. The image would produce a powerful effect upon me, and soon I felt relaxed.

Is this escapism? Frankly, it is; but what's wrong with a little escapism now and then if it helps? Sleep and entertainment are also escape valves and they are essential to our well-being. Indeed, we need to escape sometimes from the rapid pace of modern life, whether in the form of an annual vacation which removes us physically from stress and strain or a vacation in the soul for a few moments each day when we retreat into a quiet room in our mind.

When utilizing a computer, before tackling a new problem the operator must first clear the prior problem from the mechanism. Otherwise, carryover of the old problem into the new one will produce an incorrect answer.

Similarly, we must clear our internal mechanism in a quiet room of our mind, rooting out irrelevance and negation and paving the way for a renewal of positive energy and determined goal-striving.

Before a plastic surgery operation, I sharpen my concentration as a preparatory measure, relaxing for a short period in the quiet room in my mind, clearing out all excess mental baggage in advance of the surgical procedure.

You must do this too. Retreat from life's pressures and tensions every day for a while into a quiet room in your mind. Refuse to buckle under stress; refuse to crumble under the impact of crisis. Do not, like so many people, falter and fall by the wayside, nerves shattered, mind reeling. Refresh yourself; then return to confront life's challenges.

Where do you start? In the quiet room of your mind, the playhouse of your mind, the theater of your mind. Call it what you will. Here's where you eliminate crippling tension and prepare to move forward—in heavy traffic, but living with it—toward your objectives.

One final point: your main purpose is not to escape permanently from stress but to escape temporarily, and then to return to face your challenges.

Therefore, you certainly do not wish to become a member of Mañana Unlimited.

Mañana Unlimited? A tomorrow-oriented organization. Or, more accurately, an organization dedicated to putting things off until tomorrow, or the day after tomorrow— or never.

There is no limit to the delaying tactics of the membership of Mañana Unlimited. Charter members will seek employment on the morrow—and have announced this pious intention during decades of unemployment.

The president of Mañana Unlimited is a decision-making functionary who has never made a decision. The other officials boast equally unblemished records.

When life's pressures become too severe, you must

escape for a moment into the quiet room of your mind. Refresh yourself with this brief daily vacation, but do not join the self-sabotaging Mañana Unlimited.

You must learn to function under stress, to hang in there under pressure, to live with crisis. Do so with tranquillity, but not at the price of accepting philosophies leading to failure.

Here is another interesting letter. This one is from a man residing in Manchester, England:

Dear Dr. Maltz,

Three years ago, my wife, while in Toronto, came across your book *Psycho-Cybernetics*. I found the book in her study. I have now read it, and I am writing to congratulate you on the success I have obtained through it, particularly chapter 12, page 172—"Do-It-Yourself Tranquilizers."

For the past twenty years, biting and picking my nails has been a real problem. With the job that I do, a good presentation of the physical is most important. Hair, face, dress, nails etc., etc. The one eyesore on my person was my nails. No matter what action I took, I always reverted to this: picking and biting. They were shocking! Then I came across your book and in chapter 12 I found something called relaxation, Pavlov's theory, and one or two items that helped me. I found that something happened inside my physical being; I responded by chewing my nails. So what did I do? When I received this message, I responded by just relaxing and then had no wish to bite my nails. As simple as that! Just like a car responds when you put it in gear! My nails are now a good length, and the desire to ill-treat them has gone.

My thanks for your wonderful book.

> Yours faithfully,
> *Barry Podmore*

Now a letter from a man in Chicago:

Dear Dr. Maltz:

The study of your writings has been a revelation and I thank you for the understanding you have given me. Your pen is indeed a scalpel in carving away emotional disfigurements of long standing.

The best to you.

Sincerely,
Harry S. K.

GUIDELINES

1. The richest, most satisfying experience of your life can be your growing acquaintanceship with the creative you.

2. Recognize that even the most successful people must endure stress and problems.

3. When you feel tense, let your imagination give you the big lift.

4. Your most important reconstructive task: turning self-doubt into self-confidence.

5. Stress is part of living; stand up to it.

6. Procrastination means tension.

7. Cure internal myopia; see the best in yourself, not the worst.

Principles to Live By

1. Use tensions as stimuli to provide you with rich creative opportunity.

2. Fight off resistance to worthwhile plans, rejecting self-imprisonment in favor of a voyage to the golden land of relaxation.

3. Exercise creative aggressiveness to reach your goal without injuring others; arrogant destructive aggressiveness, never.

4. Remember, negation as a way of life cannot bring tranquillity.

5. Get off the fence of indecision; you find peace when you make up your mind and move toward your goal.

6. Transform fear and disbelief into courage and conviction.

7. Don't permit pressure to tie you into knots. You are capable of rising above it.

8. Keep in mind that loneliness and tranquillity cannot coexist; no one can make you lonely without your consent.

9. Work actively for peace of mind.

10. In times of extreme irritation, feel compassion for yourself and for others.

11. Remove the scars created by negative thinking. Live in the present. Remember that peace of mind means now.

12. Forget Yesterday Incorporated. It is a bankrupt organization. Resign, and look for inner peace today.

EXERCISE

On paper or mirror, write the word "EVOLUTON" and say to yourself:

"I embark on a new career. My objective? The evolution of me from tension to tone, from irritation to tranquillity, from resistance to relaxation. Accepting my imperfections, tolerating my weaknessess, I will grow stronger. I will move toward positive feelings and goals, moving away from negation. My growth involves evolution, not revolution. I will strive to rise above my inner riotousness, my internal rock-throwing, my chronic resentment, each day formulating worthwhile goals and moving toward them, insisting on the peaceful evolution of me."

Thoughts to Live By

1. *When you stop making mistakes, you stop growing.*

In plain language, the individual who never commits a blunder never takes a chance.

2. *Uncertainty and fear are blind areas of the mind.* Exercise foresight and rise above uncertainty and fear.

Chapter 13

Name of the Game:
Crisis into Creative Opportunity

Sure, it's a hard life for many people. I agree readily that existence seems to involve an endless array of problems, to which there are not always easy solutions. Crisis is around the corner. At any moment, no matter how smoothly your plans are proceeding, the unexpected can sweep in with an uppercut that will drive you to your knees.

Then what? Then, my friends, notwithstanding old age or a teetering job, financial disaster or declining health, you must call on your internal resources, grouping them with fortitude and determination. With boldness and ingenuity you must meet the crisis head on.

In fact, this is the name of the game of life. Shiver and shake before the impact of crisis, and you are a loser. Stand up to crisis, resolutely, intelligently, undauntedly, and you can become a winner.

You can, moreover, turn a crisis into a creative opportunity; and that's what this chapter is all about.

Now, in the playhouse of your mind, seat yourself and visualize this dramatization.

CASE HISTORY

[NARRATOR: The young woman in the consultation room is sobbing bitterly. The doctor says nothing; after a while, she wipes the tears from her face with a tissue.]

DOCTOR: What is your name?

WOMAN: Jeanette.

DOCTOR: Your age?

JEANETTE: Twenty-four.

DOCTOR: Are you from New York?

JEANETTE: No, Los Angeles.

DOCTOR: What's your problem?

JEANETTE: I'm confused.

DOCTOR: About what?

JEANETTE: Well, it's my job mostly that's bothering me.

DOCTOR: What is your job?

JEANETTE: I work for the advertising department of a magazine.

DOCTOR: Why does this job bother you?

JEANETTE: I don't get along well with the other people.

DOCTOR: Is this your fault?

JEANETTE: No. If I don't stick up for myself, they walk all over me. If I do, they argue with me. Either way it's a crisis every day.

DOCTOR: Who are the other people?

JEANETTE: The girls on my level, clerical personnel.

DOCTOR: What does your boss think of you?

JEANETTE: Oh, he says I shouldn't let other people push me around.

DOCTOR: In other words, he's with you and he doesn't want you to leave?

JEANETTE: No. He wants me to stay.

DOCTOR: How do you feel about it?

JEANETTE: Sometimes I feel like flying home.

DOCTOR: Will this solve your problem?

JEANETTE: No, but my boss's boss wants him to fire me because I'm not punctual. And, for some reason, the harder I press to get to work on time, the longer it takes me. Today I didn't get there at all.

DOCTOR: Tell me, do you feel superior to the other girls?

JEANETTE: Oh no.

DOCTOR: Do you like the job?

JEANETTE: I love it.

DOCTOR: What is more important, the job or the people who are upsetting you?

JEANETTE: The people.

DOCTOR: I can't see that. Your job is more important. The attitudes of these people cannot be as basic.

JEANETTE: Would I feel upset by people on any job, or is it just these people?

DOCTOR: I don't know, but this I can tell you: If you leave this job without fighting for your rights, you will have to face this same kind of problem again.

JEANETTE: Then it's not the job?

DOCTOR: It's you.

JEANETTE: What's wrong with me?

DOCTOR: You're too timid, and you don't think enough of yourself.

JEANETTE: I guess you're right.

DOCTOR: Tell yourself that you're somebody, somebody important.

JEANETTE: I wish I could feel that way.

DOCTOR: You must find yourself, your real true self-image.

JEANETTE: My real self?

DOCTOR: Yes.

JEANETTE: I remember; that's in your book.

DOCTOR: Fine, but have you lived it?

JEANETTE: I try to think positively.

DOCTOR: Psycho-cybernetics is positive doing. You helped create your own crisis; now turn this crisis into a creative opportunity.

JEANETTE: How?

DOCTOR: During periods of tension, relax and think clearly about what you're doing. Smile instead of gritting your teeth. Move toward self-reliance instead of building mountains out of molehills. Cool it when others try to irritate you. That's first in standing up to a period of crisis.

JEANETTE: I remember that's in your book.

DOCTOR: Then let it be in your mind and your heart. Don't you deserve it?

JEANETTE: Yes.

DOCTOR: Do you have a boy friend at the office?

JEANETTE: Yes.

DOCTOR: Are the other girls jealous?

JEANETTE: Yes, and they gossip.

DOCTOR: Let them.

JEANETTE: When I'm happy, they get mad.

DOCTOR: So what?

JEANETTE: I keep a flower on my desk.

DOCTOR: Do they resent this?

JEANETTE: Yes.

DOCTOR: Ignore them; keep it there.

JEANETTE: Sometimes I feel like quitting.

DOCTOR: Worst thing you could do. If they discharge you for bringing beauty into the office, it's very different from resigning. If you resign, you run away from yourself.

JEANETTE: Tell me, what should I do?

DOCTOR: Very simple. Use a flower.

JEANETTE: A flower?

DOCTOR: Yes. In time of stress, bring a flower into the office, a symbol for you to stand firm and sweet under stress.

JEANETTE: I think about revenge.

DOCTOR: Don't! It's not a question of getting revenge, but of getting over timidity. Your shyness sustains your feeling of being nobody. Take courage, and bring beauty into your crisis.

JEANETTE: Is that all?

DOCTOR: Improve your self-image and live up to your dignity. Every now and then, buy a flower on your way to the office. Go to the mirror and say to yourself, "I play a fine role before the mirror, reacting creatively to crisis in my place of work by putting it in true perspective, by relaxing under pressure, by confronting challenges and enhancing my self-respect. My motto shall be *fight* instead of *flight* because I am fighting for my dignity." Now take the flower and return to the mirror, saying to yourself with a smile, "I deserve this flower because I refuse to humble myself. I refuse to be inferior. From now on, I shall build my self-image. I came into this world to succeed, and succeed I will because I deserve it."

JEANETTE: What have I got to lose?

DOCTOR: Nothing, and you have plenty to gain.

JEANETTE: Right.

[NARRATOR: The doctor did not hear from Jeanette for a year or so, but one day she phoned him.]

JEANETTE: Do you know who this is? It's Jeanette.

DOCTOR: Good to hear from you, Jeanette. How are you?

JEANETTE: Great.

DOCTOR: Still on the same job?

JEANETTE: Oh no. I quit a long time ago.

DOCTOR: You weren't fired?

JEANETTE: No. The flower exercise worked. Suddenly, I began to realize my own worth. Instead of worrying about other people, I found myself starting to appreciate what I could give to the world.

DOCTOR: You sound far away.

JEANETTE: I'm in California, Los Angeles. I have a job as assistant manager for an advertising firm.

DOCTOR: Wonderful.

JEANETTE: You see, I got the job by being different. I always came to the office with two great weapons: a flower and a smile.

DOCTOR: Do you ever take a flower to your own home?

JEANETTE: Once a month. I call it Mirror Night.

HOMEWORK

What would you consider the most formidable crisis that could confront you? Think hard.

Thoughts on possible crises:

A business crisis comparable to that of the thirties.

Terminal cancer.

Driving a car down a steep hill and discovering that the brakes don't work.

Appearing totally unprepared before a group of colleagues.

Being on stage, nervous, no place to hide from a thousand eyes and more.

Failing in health and becoming dependent upon other people.

Feeling on the verge of death.

Experiencing the abrupt conviction that there is no God, and that the universe has no real purpose.

Losing all sense of communication with family members.

QUESTIONS AND ANSWERS

Q. What is the difference between an individual who crumbles in an emergency and one who rallies?

A. The latter has learned how to cope with emergencies.

Q. How do we learn to cope with crises?

A. Mastering skills under noncrisis conditions.
Reacting positively rather than negatively.
Seeing them in proper perspective.

Q. How can one learn skills without pressure?

A. Mainly by shadowboxing, using as aids a mirror, dry runs, and other forms of practice exercises.

Q. How can a person learn to react positively rather than negatively?

A. Plan a constructive course of action rather than worry passively.
Accept the challenge and determine to assert our strength.
Assume an attitude of confidence rather than fear.
Keep in mind a positive objective.

Q. What if we respond creatively?

A. The emergency reactivates a flow of reserve power. The excitement is reinforcing.

Q. Can excitement work for good?

A. In flight, it will gear us to run.
If we choose to fight, it will boost our sense of power.

Q. How can one apply perspective to evaluating a crisis?

A. Be realistic; don't exaggerate or overreact. Ask yourself what is the worst thing that could happen.

Remember that failure does not mean death. Ask yourself what you can lose if you do your best.

Crisis Control Plus

We might call this chapter "Crisis Control Plus," because the key idea is that first we move to cope with the pressure situation, bringing it under control; then we go beyond this to turn negative into positive, seeking out a fresh opportunity for growth.

The point is this: the winners in this world must build the capacity to deal competently with emergency situations. If they cannot do this, a competitor will move in and pick up the chips.

Learning skills is not enough. The minor leagues are crammed with highly talented baseball players who choke up under pressure; the golfer who places forty-first or fifty-second in a big tournament may be able to drive the ball farther than the winner, but can he sink a ten-foot putt when all the marbles are up for grabs?

Bright students are common enough, but the question is whether they can demonstrate their aptitude under the pressure of an important examination. Deft salesmen are also no rarity, but can they allow their skills to surface when a huge prize is at stake? Many women are gifted conversationalists, but will the sparkling chatter flow free upon a crucial social occasion?

In other words—and let's relate this to you—the question is: Can you control a crisis, or do you let a crisis control you? Rephrased, can you turn a crisis into a creative opportunity? Are you a "money player" or do you fall to pieces in the clutch?

To perform at peak under emergency conditions, we must (1) practice without crisis, (2) respond positively to the crisis situation, (3) see these situations in realistic perspective.

1. *Practice without crisis.* Master essential skills when the pressure is not terrifying, when you can concentrate on what you have to absorb, when you can relax as you grow. It wouldn't make sense to teach yourself to swim by overtaking a sinking ship in a jet, parachuting aboard, and then leaping into the water as the ship exploded, praying that somehow you would manage to propel your way through the freezing water even though you'd never taken a single swimming lesson. Of course not. Obviously, you would learn the art of swimming in advance, practice without pressure, and learn under carefully monitored circumstances.

The same principle applies generally. You learn how to deal with crisis in noncrisis situations, pacing yourself gently, practicing without stress, taking advantage of "dry runs," shadowboxing before you climb through the ropes into the ring.

Shadowboxing is most helpful in this respect. You wage your fight in your imagination before the real emergency presents itself. You learn the right moves in your mind and, as you see yourself fighting the good fight successfully, your image of yourself improves. Then, you are better prepared to launch yourself into the most trying situations.

2. *Respond positively to the crisis situation.* Rise above your timidity and apprehensiveness to aggressiveness and a sense of purpose. Keep your goal firmly in mind. Stop running away; move forward.

One danger is that you may mistake excitement for fear. But they are not identical. Any crisis may bring on excitement; accept this feeling and keep moving forward toward your goal. Some of the most professional actors channel their excitement and utilize it to give a stunning performance. The same applies to the combat soldier; he uses his excitement to harness his aggression effectively against the enemy.

Stop fearing challenges. If you like yourself—in defeat as well as in victory—you will mobilize your prime assets to deal with challenge.

3. *See crises in perspective.* Too many people magnify danger to the point that they render themselves helpless during hard times. They make mountains out of mole-hills and see disaster everywhere. With such a mental attitude, they never have a chance.

You must learn to face emergencies with a positive attitude, seeing them in perspective, asking yourself what is the worst thing that could happen, fighting the tendency to dissolve into hysterical flight.

Remember that you are not alone in your fear of crisis. Great men like Bertrand Russell and Thomas Carlyle had to rise above inner self-doubt and cowardice to find internal courage to sustain them in times of threat and danger. Although with difficulty, they were able to do this.

Discard a "life-or-death" attitude before you shrink into a dark shell inside yourself and give up on all worthwhile goals. Very seldom will it be "do or die." In your mind it may be so, but rarely in reality.

There's an interesting story about Walter Pidgeon, the supremely confident-looking actor. He was terrified during his premier public performance and failed miserably at the start. Between acts, however, he reasoned with himself that he had already flopped, so what did he have to lose? His fear vanished, and he rallied splendidly. He had won his battle and was on his way.

Two more suggestions for dealing with crises:

1. *Build your self-image.* The more you like yourself,

the more you will be able to realize that the crisis is mainly in your mind.

2. *Use your imagination as a friend.* This is a blessed weapon; use it positively. If you are in command of the inner space of your imagination, chances are that you will gain control of the outer space where you encounter and master crisis.

Here's a letter from a man in the insurance business; my ideas helped him.

I must tell you something that happened to me that you'll appreciate. About six years ago, I became so depressed and confused, that I came close to jumping off the roof of the 24th floor of the Hotel McAlpin. One of the factors that saved my life was a book that you wrote called *Psycho-Cybernetics.* That chapter "Turning a Crisis into an Opportunity" did the trick.

We are over twenty men in this insurance agency. Whenever I see anybody discouraged and confused, I tell him "read *that* book." We had a meeting last week and the subject matter was the importance of reading your famous book. Whenever I am down in the dumps, I run home and read your book. Speaking for me only, your book is magic to me and, really, my "Bible."

I look forward to meeting you in person.

Cordially,
Jack H. Fanshel

This letter came from Birmingham, Alabama.

When I was a senior in high school, my grades were terrible. I had a negative attitude toward life, and a low opinion of my own abilities. The director of the private school I was attending knew this, and recommended that I read *Psycho-Cybernetics.* I was in a state of acute depression and desperation, and although I didn't think the book would do me any good, I was ready to try anything.

I started reading the book with the attitude that it was a put-on to make a crummy writer some easy money, because he knew there were people like me, reaching out for help. I was quite surprised to find that I could identify my problem in this book—the first step in solving it.

It has been years since I read this book, and I cannot recall a great deal of the content. (I gave the book to a friend after I finished it, who in turn passed it on.) However, the thing I remember most, which solved my problem, is the fact that positive thinking and doing is the only way to bring positive results, while negative thinking only confirms in one's mind that he or she is a loser. This was the key to my problem. I turned a crisis into an opportunity. Thank you, Dr. Maltz, for writing *Psycho-Cybernetics*.

B. L.

GUIDELINES

Liabilities you can do without:

1. *Revenge.* You have been wronged. If you dwell on this for a lifetime, you will wrong yourself interminably.

2. *Envy.* Better to build your self-image than to envy those you believe are better than you.

3. *Sulkiness.* Set goals for your imperfect self in an imperfect world and you move toward creative living.

4. *Elimination from life.* No matter how old you may be, never retire from life.

5. *Narrowmindedness.* Renounce mental and spiritual myopia; be open-minded.

6. *Temper.* When you learn to control this hairtrigger temper, you move toward a new exalted status as a professional human being.

7. *Mistakes.* No one is perfect. Forgive yourself and rise above your mistakes.

8. *Hatred.* The person who hates others loathes himself. The person who respects others respects himself.

9. *Emotional negligence.* Refuse to wallow in negative feelings. Steer toward positive goals.

10. *Tension.* A debilitating habit; it is far more rewarding to make a habit of relaxation.

Principles to Live By

Seizing opportunity:

1. Realize this: *you* are opportunity. Never will it knock. You create opportunity by building confidence in yourself.

2. Stop wasting mental energy moaning about yesterday. It's fine to slow down when the red light on your mental dashboard signals, but the light will never change to green while you look backward. Look forward positively, toward new opportunities.

3. Stop, look, and listen in the present. Focus on today's goal, convinced that it is your right to succeed.

4. Stop downgrading and accept yourself; otherwise, you will never view the dawn of opportunity.

5. Set constructive goals within your capabilities.

6. Don't let crisis throw you. Stand up and fight for your rights.

7. Relax; practice without pressure.

8. Shadowbox, playing a starring role before the mirror. In your mind, deliver a knockout blow to negative feelings.

9. Surrender to compassion, not resentment; to courage, not cowardice; to assertion of assets, not liabilities.

10. Failure-oriented and success-oriented, simultaneously, you must countdown in the inner space of your mind and launch yourself toward today's opportunities.

EXERCISE

Write the word "CRISIS" on paper or mirror and deliver a "commencement" address to yourself:

"Today is the day for action. Today is an Adventure in Living. A creative mind watcher, I will turn crisis into opportunity.

"I am in the driver's seat; no one else will drive me. When, en route to my destination, I approach a dead end, I will back up, swivel around, and resume the journey toward my goal.

"It was Victor Hugo's conviction that a timely idea was more significant than military strength. What is my timely idea? To become a mind watcher. With my mind in control, I will guide myself past the roller coaster of crisis. I will survive the ups and downs, and arrive at my goal. I can see value in me, not in the sense of vanity but realizing my possibilities. Through daily practice I will implement my growth, creating a vast reservoir of internal strength available on call for crises—instant confidence."

Thoughts to Live By

1. *Faith and belief are wings.* Flapping them, you may soar through crisis to a destination of rich creative living.

2. *Take time to know your better self.* If you don't, you will live with never-ending internal crisis.

Your Greatest Need—Light

This is a true story that goes back to the days of World War II.

In Alsace-Lorraine, bordering France and Germany, advancing American infantrymen met fierce resistance from the Nazi defenders. Progress was painful, with house-to-house and hand-to-hand battles, and there were intelligence reports that the enemy would counterattack.

At dusk, an American staff sergeant and his squad occupied a house on the edge of a main street. They preceded the main body of United States troops and kept a nervous lookout for a possible counterattack. Soon their visibility was gone; and, although there was no indication of hostile forces in the area, the sergeant posted guards at each window.

This was a thankless assignment in the dark, but one sentry said he thought he heard rustling noises outside in the street.

Immediately, the sergeant contacted headquarters on his walkie-talkie, and they ordered a flare.

In an instant the sky was illuminated and there, frozen like statues in the pierced blackness, were dozens of German soldiers, poised to attack the Americans' house. Panicking, they scrambled back behind cover on the other side of the street.

Then an all-night vigil began. Systematically, the sergeant organized a series of continual harassing techniques: flares to light up the darkness, intermittent rifle fire into the thoroughfare, and volleys of grenades exploding ominously. Until dawn, without letup, these improvised measures kept the Germans off guard and, with the return of visibility, they still had not attacked. And they never did, because another squad of American infantrymen, armed with flamethrowers, took them prisoner that morning.

Why should I recite a war story? It's a story about opportunity. It's about illuminating *your* enemy, negative feelings, before you can turn a crisis into a creative opportunity. It's about your personal campaign to outflank your enemy, placing your negative feelings on the defensive, so you can counterattack and move upon your goals.

Your greatest need is light to penetrate *your* inner darkness, to reveal your sabotaging inner forces so that you can survive crisis and seize opportunity.

Chapter 14

Reaching Goals Makes You a Winner

Winning and goals go together. Remember, winning implies forward movement and sense of purpose. You can't win by wandering aimlessly around in circles.

The winner in life formulates goals that are worthwhile for him. He achieves them by rising above self-doubt and inhibition to realize his full potential as a human being.

Once again, seat yourself in the playhouse of your mind as we unfold a real-life dramatization of a loser struggling to become a winner.

CASE HISTORY

[NARRATOR: Robert, a slim-looking man of forty-five, faces the doctor in his consultation room. Although he tries to look poised, he cannot conceal his tension.]

ROBERT: Your book *Psycho-Cybernetics* has influenced me profoundly.

DOCTOR: Thank you.

ROBERT: May I ask how long it took to write?

DOCTOR: Well, thirty years thinking, and about three years writing.

ROBERT: It's like a bible to me.

DOCTOR: How did it help you?

ROBERT: In many ways. For many years I was a fighter pilot in the Air National Guard.

DOCTOR: When did you read it?

ROBERT: Oh, around 1961, I guess.

DOCTOR: But you became a pilot because of *your* desire, not because of *my* book.

ROBERT: It helped, though.

DOCTOR: In what way?

ROBERT: My thinking was negative, and I would criticize myself for making mistakes. You made me understand that you can't succeed *except* by rising above mistakes.

DOCTOR: What impressed you most in the book?

ROBERT: That your self-image underlies change, that if you can strengthen your self-image you can feel confident and become a winner.

DOCTOR: Anything else?

ROBERT: That the mind cannot differentiate between an actual successful experience and one vividly imagined.

DOCTOR: What do you consider the most important section of the book?

ROBERT: A number of things. Becoming self-reliant, relaxing by living in the present, seeing yourself at your best not your worst, keeping up with yourself: all those things.

DOCTOR: Which chapter did you like best?

ROBERT: The chapter on building that winning feeling. The understanding that confidence is a quality you build yourself from within, and that nobody can hand it to you on a silver platter. *You* are confidence. Using the positive glow of past successes, you move toward your goal today. You remove the old record of failure and place a new recording of success on the phonograph.

DOCTOR: You are a true disciple.

ROBERT: I am not alone. Many commercial airline pilots join me.

DOCTOR: That's good to hear. But, tell me, why did you come to see me?

ROBERT: I have a problem.

DOCTOR: Tell me about it.

ROBERT: Well, I don't really know where to begin. I teach pilots to fly. That is, I teach older pilots to fly jet planes.

It's sometimes a difficult transition from propeller planes to jet planes. I have also trained a group of rookie pilots fresh out of school. Today most of them are doing well, getting the job done. I have a knack of simplifying complexity.

DOCTOR: Fine, but what's the problem?

ROBERT: I've been grounded. I can't fly any more.

DOCTOR: Why?

ROBERT: I participated in an air combat maneuver not too long ago. I suffered a whiplash injury when the violent upward thrust of the craft flung my neck forward.

DOCTOR: Weren't you treated for this?

ROBERT: Yes, but the pain is still quite severe in the cervical vertebrae, fifth and sixth. I was forced to stop flying.

DOCTOR: Since when?

ROBERT: The last six months. I'm a colonel, but I can't get back to flying, and that's my problem. Your book helped me then, but how can it help me now?

DOCTOR: It can still help.

ROBERT: How?

DOCTOR: First you must help yourself. There's an old Irish proverb that goes something like this: "If God shuts one door, he opens another." But where are you? On the floor, looking up to God, saying, "Take me out of this misery"? Or do you stand poised, feet on the ground, hand on the door, ready to open it when opportunity knocks?

ROBERT: Which do you think?

DOCTOR: You tell me. But, first, remember that you are opportunity and that you win by turning crisis into opportunity. You believed this before and lived this before. Live this way now.

ROBERT: But how?

DOCTOR: Are you good at communications?

ROBERT: Sure.

DOCTOR: You were a teacher. You said you were a first-rate flying instructor.

ROBERT: Yes.

DOCTOR: Isn't psycho-cybernetics a form of flying too?

ROBERT: I don't understand.

DOCTOR: Psycho-cybernetics is flying, mentally and spiritually. You soar toward your destination on wings of hope and belief. Flying physically in a plane, you were, psycho-cybernetically speaking, flying mentally and spiritually. Now, frustrated, despairing, you are grounded physically, mentally, and spiritually. But in the latter two senses, you can still fly.

ROBERT: How?

DOCTOR: By helping other people get off the ground.

ROBERT: How can I do that?

DOCTOR: Through psycho-cybernetics. Would you like to teach lost goalless people in workshops? Would you like to instruct them in mental and spiritual flying procedures? Would you like to help them find their self-respect?

ROBERT: Yes.

DOCTOR: What do you say?

ROBERT: Sure; I'd love it!

DOCTOR: I think you'll do fine.

ROBERT: You're giving me a new lease on life, Doctor.

DOCTOR: No, you're giving it to yourself. You've been a winner before; you can do it again.

HOMEWORK

What is a truly worthwhile goal?

Thoughts on goals:

To function effectively in the world.

To build the courage to be an individual.

To give with brotherliness to others.

To stand up for what is right.

To strive to reach the fullest potential.

To formulate an important goal every day.

To build sound mental and physical health.

To live each day fully—as if it were the last day on earth.

To be true to myself.

To forgive and forget.

To understand and communicate with others.

To harness excitement to goals rather than to useless emotional eruptions.

To learn to accept rationally the many minor problems in daily living.

To throw away the mask and aspire to display the real personality.

To live with wisdom and common sense instead of with unreason and poor temperament.

To learn that personal success is tied to helping others achieve too.

To develop a workable standard of values.

To accept the possibility of positive change and work toward it.

To practice honesty as a way of life.

To seek self-respect every day.

To win out over frustration, resentment, and emptiness.

To seize creative opportunity.

To win the war against negative feelings.

To find peace of mind.

To conquer loneliness.

To build friendship by offering friendship.

To live creatively at sixty-five and over.

To live dynamically every day.

To develop the smile principle.

To find the action in myself.

To evolve as a creative mind watcher.

To say to myself, when things are tough, "No matter what, I'm with me."

QUESTIONS AND ANSWERS

Q. Under what circumstance is our automatic mechanism most effective?

A. When given specific goals.

Q. How should one program these goals?

A. By picturing end results.

Q. Why concentrate on goal-striving, in terms of ways and means?

A. To avoid blocking the mechanism.

Q. How can the mechanism provide the means?

A. Through sharply defined objectives.

Q. How does one give sharp definition to goals?

A. By visualizing end results clearly.

Q. When we are anxious, fearful, and humiliated, what is our goal?

A. Failure.

Q. How does the nervous system respond to a real experience as opposed to a vividly imagined one?

A. There is no difference.

Q. Why is this so?

A. The nervous system responds to what it *believes* is true. It will react to vivid images of either failure or success.

Q. How can we be sure we are moving toward our desired objective?

A. We feel that winning glow.

Q. What reactivates the functioning of the automatic success mechanism, in addition to sharply defined objectives?

A. A feeling of confidence.

Q. Does the winning feeling *cause* successful functioning?

A. No; but, since we know we are on the way to success, we feel confident.

Q. How do we gain this feeling of success when we need it?

A. By defining the objective, then feeling that we will assuredly achieve this goal.

Q. Who are some examples of people with this winning feeling?

A. Dave Stockton—golf.
   Wes Parker—baseball.
   Don Chandler—football.
   J. C. Penney—marketing.
   Henry Kaiser—industry.
   Les Giblin—public relations.

Q. What generally accompanies the winning feeling?

A. Realistic winning in the everyday world.

Q. How do we acquire the success habit?

A. By participating in activities at which we believe we can succeed.

Q. Will this prevent us from tackling difficult problems?

A. Not if we can develop the capacity to tolerate our failures.

Q. How do we acquire this winning feeling?

A. Through beginning with tasks at which we can succeed, then tackling more difficult tasks.

Q. How does one improve a considerable skill?

A. Stop pressing.

Q. How do we strengthen the impact of built-in success patterns?

A. See them vividly in your mind.

Q. Will dwelling on past successes cause us to live too much in the past?

A. Not if we bring this good feeling into the present and live it today.

Q. What is a technique for utilizing the power of imagination constructively?

A. Instead of agonizing over yesterday's failures, visualize possibilities of total, assured, inevitable success.

Q. Should we force belief in success?

A. No. Start with the feeling of possibility.

Q. What brings on feelings of failure?

A. Basically, dwelling on past failures instead of past successes.

Q. What can we do with feelings of failure?

A. Ignore them or accept them.

Q. How can we benefit from failure feelings?

A. The power generated by these feelings can be transferred into positive action.

Q. How should we respond to other people's negative opinions of us?

A. These opinions can motivate us into taking aggressive positive action.

Q. How can we control our feelings?

A. Indirectly.

Q. How?

A. By replacing negative thoughts and images with positive wholesome feelings and images.

Q. What is the effect of concentrating upon negative feelings?

A. It reinforces them, makes them stronger.

Q. Suppose we drive them out of our mind?

A. Other worries replace them if the emotional attitude remains negative.

Q. How can we replace evil with good?

A. By use of positive imaging.

Q. Why do we worry?

A. Out of habit.

Q. What is the effect of habitual worry?

A. It makes us tense and miserable.

Q. What if worry serves as a signal to practice remembering past successes or to anticipate the joy of future successes?

A. This eliminates the worry.

Q. What if we help others to get a winning feeling and strengthen their image of themselves?

A. We bolster our own image.

Q. What memories can we choose to recall?

A. Successes or failures.

Q. What can we do with failure memories?

A. We can modify them with our current thinking patterns, refusing to torture ourselves with them.

Q. Why should we ignore failure memories?

A. Disuse weakens their impact.

Q. What about feelings of personal responsibility when we develop the capacity to change our recollections of yesterday?

A. No longer defeated by the past, we are able to deal with responsibility and chart the future.

Q. What about our "phonograph"?

A. We can continue to play the same old broken record of yesterday, or we can change the tune, playing a new record today.

That Winning Kick

Former Green Bay Packer place-kicker Don Chandler said this about my theory of creative psycho-cybernetics: "It makes you know what you can do, what you have inside of you, and knowing that you are better able to bring it out."

Tennis star Cliff Richey has used psycho-cybernetics to win, and an imposing list of top athletes have employed it to give them confidence under fire. They include a number of pro football players and baseball players. Among them are former greats Bart Starr and Jerry Kramer, in football, and big leaguers Mike Epstein and Bill Singer in baseball. Many golfers also swear by psycho-cybernetics. One is Dave Stockton, who credits my theories with helping him win in the tense competitive tournament atmosphere. Actors and actresses have used the principles of psycho-cybernetics to help them endure the pressures of performing; so have executives, salesmen, ministers, teachers, men and women in all walks of life.

But you may ask, "How can I feel like a winner when I've always been a loser?"

The key word here is "always." Everybody knows what it feels like to lose and many people are accustomed to losing. But, "always"? No, no, no.

This is a very important point because all you need to build on from the past is the feel of success, and you can make even one success go a long way.

How? By bringing this feeling of success powerfully into your mind, retaining it there to grow. Then you can launch yourself toward new objectives with a sense of internal fortification.

Here's a program for building that winning feeling.

1. *Build your self-image.* Become a friend to yourself by learning to rise above negative feelings and appreciating your virtues. Forgive your mistakes and bury them in the tomb of time. You're only human. See yourself realistically, but at your best. Keep working to strengthen this new friendly picture of yourself. See yourself with kind eyes, picturing your past achievements, savoring the old success feelings, feeding your imagination with these wonderful moments. Make the image of success live in your mind. Manufacture this rich feeling; it is your prime product.

2. *Formulate worthwhile goals.* Take courage and set goals for which you can feel a real enthusiasm, but also make sure that they are within your capabilities. Limit the number of goals you formulate to avoid confusion and, if possible, set one basic goal a day.

3. *Move toward your goals.* With your self-image strong, with your objectives sharply outlined, you are crouched, ready, awaiting the signal of the starter's gun. Then, go! Your strong image of yourself sets in operation your success mechanism and, as you advance upon your cherished objectives, you will feel the glow of confidence, that is the winning feeling, and you feel it in your bones.

Reaching goals makes you feel like a winner, but it all starts with your self-image, because first you must feel that you're worth it. It's a tough life, and you have to feel tough enough to stand up for yourself under pressure.

Easy? No, but you can do it. Lecturing throughout this

country, I get to chat with a lot of people and sense their determination to build meaningful lives for themselves and their loved ones. People with defective hearts and missing limbs, old people and young people, fighting to overcome their handicaps and move toward their goals. Men in penitentiaries struggle to build their inner resources in their hunger to "get ahead" when their sentence has been served. As ex-convicts, they do not forget this resolve, but use the principles of psycho-cybernetics to carve out a new life.

One of my own goals was to become an effective public speaker, as I have related in another book, *Creative Living for Today*. After some time, many came to look upon me as a "born orator," but actually I was at first quite shy. How did I develop the capacity to make public appearances and handle myself in the spotlight? By winning the war against my negative feelings, concentrating on positive goals, reactivating the functioning of my success mechanism, then moving briskly toward my objectives.

Here is a letter I received from a hockey player.

I have played quite a few years of ice hockey . . . in both Canada and the United States. I have never had a disappointing season except for this winter. It seemed that everything I did worked against me. I could not score goals or make passes. I couldn't even concentrate on playing a good game. I went through fifty games of agony, pressing harder and harder to play well and score goals, but to no avail. My season's output was a lousy six goals in fifty games. I was on the verge of quitting the game even though I knew my conditioning was good and my body strong. My position on the team was uncertain. I had not produced, but I wanted to play for the United States World Hockey Team in the world games held in Vienna, Austria.

A business associate of mine, in a casual conversation, mentioned the book *Psycho-Cybernetics* and how it improved his thinking. He recommended it to me and I bought it with the idea that it might help my hockey career as well as business.

I immediately began applying the techniques to improve myself. I sat down in my lounge chair each day in my office and turned the lights off. I reenacted as many situations in as many games as I could remember, especially in the games when I failed miserably. I discovered that in almost every game that I recalled, I distinctly remembered experiencing great emotional fear of being injured while playing. As a matter of fact this fear seemed to dominate every situation that I could recall. The answer to my difficulties seemed so simple to me as I sat in that dark room. Why, I was constantly thinking of being injured and this preoccupation of my mind was enough to throw my entire game into failure after failure.

I immediately began to replace this negative feeling and thought with a positive feeling and thought. I recalled every situation in the past when I had done well and had scored goals. I relived the excitement and the great feeling of being a winner, when I scored those goals. I replaced these thoughts, eliminating the fear of injury.

I honestly repeated this system each and every day through February and March. Things did not change immediately but I knew in my mind that they would—and change they did! I moved from my bench position as a reserve to the starting lineup. I began scoring goals and playing the game with new enthusiasm. It seemed as if I had never played the game before. My success was unbelievable. My name appeared in headlines. I kept scoring the winning goals where two months back I could not do the job. An amazing turnabout. I continued to lead the team in scoring with eight big goals during the European tournaments, most of them key goals which won the games. Soon it will be the Olympic year and I know exactly what I am going to do to be on that team.

Here is another interesting letter from a young woman serving in the United States Army, stationed in Texas:

Dear Dr. Maltz,

I am sure that you know the results of psycho-cybernetics with patients you actually see and consult. I thought perhaps you would be interested in how your book *Psycho-Cybernetics* affected me.

The first copy of the book was purchased in 1963. At that time, I was twenty-two years old, weighed approximately 276 pounds, had a mediocre job, and was a classic victim of a "failure" mechanism. Unfortunately, I was "agnostic" if I could use the term toward psycho-cybernetics. Nothing ever went right for me, so why should that work? What I needed was a "miracle."

In the winter of 1968, I went into a "Weight-Watcher" class. This is one of the finest organizations of its kind. Whether deliberately or unconsciously this organization uses goal-striving techniques. If I was referring in my mind to your book I'll never know; but I constructed *in detail* in my mind a vision of a thin girl. When I had lost about forty pounds, the lecturer at one of the Weight Watcher meetings mentioned *Psycho-Cybernetics* as recommended reading. I returned home and got out my copy: "the truth shall set you free."

Rereading, or should I say really reading your book for the first time, I realized literally how important your writings were. The results of Weight Watchers and *Psycho-Cybernetics* was a weight loss of 122 pounds.

But your book helped me reach another goal. Having achieved a new physical image I sought more gainful employment. But I became bored. I reasoned that I was bored with life when fat but I couldn't possibly be bored as a thin person.

Deep down inside I knew there was something I always wanted to do. But, of course, my weight kept me from it. That goal was reached and I decided to try for a new one.

237

I can now proudly say I am a member of the Women's Army Corps. One year ago, this did not seem like a possibility. I visited the recruiting office for all the branches of the services. I read each brochure and knew in every fiber of my being that this was what I wanted.

Getting into the position of being able to write to you on army stationery was a great challenge. First off, I was twenty-eight years old. I was too old for the Navy and Air Force, but within limits for the Women Marines and Womens Army Corps. Since the army had a guaranteed enlistment program, I chose them.

The next obstacle was the qualifying test. Perhaps you have heard that the army takes just any one. Not so. To qualify, one must score a minimum of 51 points. The first time I tested I scored 41. The next time only 43.

Needless to say, I hired a math tutor and faithfully each night I did two things: read a chapter in *Psycho-Cybernetics*, then studied my multiplication tables.

Again I "visualized," imagined, and put myself in uniform to reach my goal. On the third testing, I scored 51 points.

The day I went to the recruiting office, I had a copy of *Psycho-Cybernetics* in my hand. My recruiter seemed amazed because your book *Psycho-Cybernetics* is required reading for the course the United States Army gives its recruiters.

I am now rereading my fourth copy of your book. It seems I get so enthused about it, I end up giving my copy away. I am now stationed at Fort Hood, Texas. Should you lecture in Dallas or at the University of Texas at Austin, I would be interested in hearing you.

I refer to your book as "my other bible" because it has helped me so much.

Respectfully,
Pvt. Kathleen P. Rehm

GUIDELINES

Oscar Wilde said, "The fatality of good resolutions is that they are always too late."

We say, "A creative resolution is not a wish but an opportunity. It is never too late to turn a resolution into a worthwhile performance."

1. Discard negation and embark on an adventure of self-fulfillment now.

2. See yourself reaching your goal.

3. Create your own opportunity today.

4. Use your imagination for assessing your resources, courage, confidence.

5. Discipline yourself toward achievement.

6. Reach one goal, start toward another.

Principles to Live By

1. Reach for today's opportunities, forgetting yesterday's blunders. Set one goal at a time.

2. Exercise your right to succeed.

3. Make yourself aware of your real potential. It is there; you must find it.

4. With courage, you leave harbor and set out after your objectives.

5. Jump the hurdles of fear and doubt.

6. Nourish your self-image daily.

7. Go forward, not backward. Stop treading water.

8. Accept your failures and rise above them to achieve your goals. But don't reach for unrealistic goals or your lifetime will be a series of failures.

EXERCISE

Relax in the playhouse of your mind and tell yourself this:

"I will struggle to live creatively by alerting myself to the ever-present peril of negative feelings. I shall attune my ears to the alarm system inside me. When the buzzer goes off, I will not panic, but will take action. I will snuff out the internal fire, then dedicate my energies to revitalizing my sense of direction, reformulating my goals.

"Then I will be ready for the big day. What day? Self-Image Day. On this day I will tear my name off the loser's list and tack it up on the winner's list. There is no trophy for this occasion, but my self-image and I will have a heart-to-heart discussion.

"I am the ruler on Self-Image Day. No confetti, parades, television hoopla, but I feel great. About what? About me. On Self-Image Day I am a winner; that's quite a goal to achieve."

Thoughts to Live By

1. *Demand results from yourself*. Someone else can't produce for you. You have to produce for yourself.

2. *Your main goal is happiness*. Other goals must be subordinate to this. Confidence is a form of happiness; that is a goal in itself.

Chapter 15

Living a Creative Day

Psycho-cybernetics is a living force. Its purpose is simple: to help you make the most of yourself and, reaching the peak of your human potential, to live the richest, fullest life that is realistic and possible.

Your final goal: to live a creative day, in your own image, as an individual among millions. In the midst of complexity, anxiety, and confusion, this is your clear purpose: a creative day.

Only one? No, but it will do for a start. When you live one creative day, then another, and another, finally you have a creative life.

CASE HISTORY

[NARRATOR: Susan seats herself opposite the doctor in the consultation room. She is slim, pale, looks tired.]

DOCTOR: Will you tell me your age?

SUSAN: If you insist. I'm forty-two.

DOCTOR: What's your problem?

SUSAN: I'm a cheat.

DOCTOR: Whom do you cheat?

SUSAN: Myself.

DOCTOR: What do you do for a living?

SUSAN: Writing.

DOCTOR: Are you successful at it?

SUSAN: Not especially.

DOCTOR: Are you married?

SUSAN: Divorced. No children.

DOCTOR: When did your problem start?

SUSAN: A long time ago. At nineteen, I wanted to do away with myself.

DOCTOR: What about your parents?

SUSAN: They were divorced when I was eight. After that, I lived with my grandparents.

DOCTOR: Did you get along with them?

SUSAN: No, I didn't like them. When they told me not to do something, I obeyed. I was not fond of living then, but I'm not really suicidal.

DOCTOR: But all your life you have been cheating yourself.

SUSAN: I think so. On many occasions I considered doing away with myself so that nobody would know this.

DOCTOR: Any other hang-ups?

SUSAN: Sure. Fear, loneliness. When things get intolerable, I begin thinking about suicide.

DOCTOR: That's your one great wish?

SUSAN: Yes, and yet I realize that it's cheating.

DOCTOR: Still, you do stay alive. Tell me about your marriage.

SUSAN: It lasted twelve years. He was a colonel. He was a good-looking man but hated people.

DOCTOR: Did he hate *you?*

SUSAN: He was always trying to tear me down. At parties, he would criticize everybody; and, after a few drinks, he would say to me: "You were spoiled by men, but I'll unspoil you." I couldn't stand him so I walked out and went to visit a friend in Bolivia, South America.

DOCTOR: And then?

SUSAN: I worked for a man in the tourist business, and then traveled to Ecuador, where I did the same kind of work. Then, suddenly, there was a revolution so I disappeared, taking off with a mule team for the jungle.

DOCTOR: Why the jungle?

SUSAN: Oh, I was sick of life. I just wanted to get away from it all.

DOCTOR: Playing with suicide again?

SUSAN: I suppose so. Killing myself in the jungle would have been no loss to humanity. Exciting, unspoiled, beautiful; that was the jungle. Uncivilized Indians were in the jungle, and I encountered a tribe of headhunters who practiced their terrifying trade to shrink the spirit of a person and evade the possibility of revenge. The women of this tribe were not hostile. Surprisingly, we respected each other.

DOCTOR: Fine, but why take the risk of living in a jungle?

SUSAN: Well, I come from a long line of pioneers. I don't know what the reason is.

DOCTOR: Did you write a book about your experiences there?

SUSAN: Why?

DOCTOR: Well, you're a writer, and you traveled to a fascinating land with which few people have had real contact. I should think that you would wish to exploit your opportunity by writing a book. Didn't this occur to you at all?

SUSAN: Well . . .

DOCTOR: You didn't write anything?

SUSAN: Just an article on contraceptive herbs used by the Indian women. Taken orally, it was effective long before discovery of the modern pill. Writing is too hard for me lately. I sit down at the typewriter, roll in some paper, and then—nothing.

DOCTOR: Sounds like you're in a jungle in your mind. Don't you want to break free from this enveloping jungle?

SUSAN: I want to be a self-supporting person.

DOCTOR: Then, write! See yourself at your best by moving toward your goals.

SUSAN: I wish I could.

DOCTOR: If you want to, you can. But, first, what do you see when you look in the mirror?

SUSAN: Well, I used to be good-looking.

DOCTOR: I mean now, what do you see in the mirror now?

SUSAN: Oh, I see a tired, bedraggled face and . . .

DOCTOR: Do you like yourself?

SUSAN: How could I?

DOCTOR: Do you respect yourself?

SUSAN: Sometimes yes, sometimes no.

DOCTOR: Do you forgive yourself for mistakes of the past?

SUSAN: I find myself apologizing, almost for my very existence.

DOCTOR: Do you want to forgive yourself?

SUSAN: Yes, but what for?

DOCTOR: You keep running away from yourself—to a remote jungle.

SUSAN: A jungle?

DOCTOR: Not in South America. You flee into a decaying jungle in your mind.

SUSAN: How can I escape this jungle?

DOCTOR: You said you were a writer.

SUSAN: Yes, and a book has been taking shape in my mind.

DOCTOR: What's it about?

SUSAN: About constructive activity. I want to tell people they must try to do constructive things—not to be like me.

DOCTOR: Try. When you do, you will burst clear of the jungle.

SUSAN: How do I start?

DOCTOR: First, you must forgive your parents, grandparents, anyone who ever wounded you. You must forget yesterday, forgive yourself, and live in the present. Then write, and you won't wish to do away with yourself; you'll feel a new strength in yourself.

SUSAN: Do I have the courage?

DOCTOR: You had the courage to bury yourself in a jungle. Now, show you have the courage to emerge from it.

SUSAN: How?

DOCTOR: Look, it may comfort you to understand that you're not the only one with this problem. Daily, millions of people rot in a jungle in their minds, neglecting their self-respect, committing mental and spiritual suicide. In the world, there is crisis—war, riot, hijacking, pollution—but our responsibility is to control the internal crisis. We must curb the pollution arising from negative feelings and rise above the headshrinking in our inner forest. As creative

244

pioneers, we can fight our way out of this jungle to find new frontiers of opportunity for fulfillment and establishment of our status as truly professional human beings.

SUSAN: I never thought of it that way.

DOCTOR: Few people do, but you must realize that you create opportunities for yourself.

SUSAN: I'll try.

DOCTOR: Write. Keep writing. You have something to say; say it today and make this a creative day. When you wake up in the morning, gear yourself to meet the challenges of this creative day. Discipline yourself to buckle down and work toward your goal. Stop cheating yourself; rise to the full measure of your capabilities.

[NARRATOR: The doctor didn't hear from Susan for over a year, but then she mailed him some articles she had written for magazine publication. Her byline was appearing regularly in a number of periodicals and the title of one selection was "The Jungle in Your Mind." In an accompanying note, she said that each day was now a fulfillment —a creative day.]

HOMEWORK

How can one stay young?
Thoughts on continued youth:
Stay young by thinking young.
Youth is an emotional attitude.
Senility bypasses those who refuse to retire from life.
The young at heart demand more of life than timid souls resigned to deterioration.
As long as a person pursues adventure, he will stay young.
Good humor and good will know no age.
A sweet thought is as inspiring at eighty-nine as it is at nineteen.
To feel alive at any age is heaven on earth.
You're neither young nor old, but a human being.

Love and tenderness are the sparkplugs which charge up our souls.

Enthusiasm is youth and boredom is senility, no matter what your age.

QUESTIONS AND ANSWERS

Q. What do we mean by the term "overbelief"?

A. A conviction which the facts as facts do not fully justify.

Q. What makes overbeliefs essential?

A. Our need to bolster our faith in our capacity to achieve goals.

Q. What assumptions underlie psycho-cybernetics?

A. That any person can modify his self-image by sharply picturing clearly defined objectives.

That we must focus on end results.

That we can repose confidence in ourselves.

That we can shed inhibitions and overprotective façades.

Q. What is the "essence of man"?

A. "Something" animating, controlling, and using the body as vehicle.

Q. What is this "something"?

A. The real personality.

Q. What power or life force feeds the real personality?

A. A form of cosmic or universal energy flows through our bodies.

Q. What is the relation of this energy to health and the process of aging?

A. The body itself has the capacity to safeguard health and to stay young.

Q. How does this life force assist with regard to health and youthfulness?

A. By aiding our adjustment to the manifold pressures of life.

Q. In what sense do emotional attitudes affect physical health?

A. Reactivation of the failure mechanism can make us physically ill.

Q. What about healing techniques?

A. Individuals who use the success mechanism heal more quickly, feel younger.

Q. Why are some patients given placebos—make-believe medicine that only humors them?

A. Placebos create an anticipation of progress, with an objective of recovery dominant in the imagination. Meantime, the great automatic servomechanism utilizes the natural healing forces of the body.

Q. Can thinking speed up the process of aging?

A. Fearing old age, a person may formulate a negative objective for the servomechanism. It is easy to accelerate decline by "retiring" from life.

Q. What about miracles of healing?

A. They may involve natural recuperative processes strengthened by great faith.

Q. If the body is self-healing, what need is there for doctors?

A. These twin forces for healing may be mutually reinforcing.

Q. How do we attain happiness?

A. By living more completely, emphasizing achievement of goals, with a spirit of brotherliness toward ourselves and others.

Q. What are six basic human needs?

A. All individuals need security, affection, creative outlet, recognition by others, self-esteem, and areas of new experience.

Q. What about a seventh need?

A. More life.

Q. What does this mean?

A. In goal-striving, we will harness this great life

power to move us toward our goals. Without objectives, we do not require this power and tend to let it fade away.

Q. Is it true that creative individuals retain more of this life force?

A. Yes. Many remain productive in their seventies, eighties, even nineties. Many creative people in the entertainment world look younger than their age.

Q. What about retirement?

A. Never retire from life.

Q. What is the most fitting image a person can hold of himself?

A. That he is living in the image of God.

Q. What is the importance of this?

A. It can provide us with a fresh source of strength. If we live in God's image, how can we destroy ourselves with feelings of inferiority?

A Creative Day Every Day

Once, some time ago, on a Saturday, I hosted a seminar in Salinas, California, and the following morning a professor of psychology from a university nearby drove my wife and me sixty miles northeast to San Jose, where I was to deliver a lecture at a church. En route, the professor lost his way and I muttered under my breath, "We need a miracle to get us there on time."

I was due at eleven o'clock, and he didn't find the right road until five minutes before the hour. At two minutes to eleven, we climbed out of the car and, out of breath, I almost exploded through the church door and into the study of the presiding minister. He looked somewhat pale, and the sight of me lurching excitedly into the room extracted a sigh of relief from him. And then I noticed a sign behind his chair: EXPECT A MIRACLE.

Addressing the congregation, I improvised a talk on

"Expect a Miracle." "Each of you," I said, "is a miracle," and I proceeded to spell out the word:

M—Movement toward a creative day.
I —Imagination zeroed in on a productive goal.
R —Relaxation in pursuit of the big you.
A—Adjustment to the realities of each day.
C—Compassion for yourself and others.
L —Living now.
E —Encouraging others to live creatively too.

Every day a miracle, a creative miracle: that is the ideal goal of psycho-cybernetics. Every day it is our responsibility to find the miracle of our potential, remembering that we came into this world to succeed, not to fail. Daily, we give to life. Giving is not losing; it is a source of internal fortification and external reinforcement. When you give, you feel young and useful and happy. Then your cup runneth over.

The first hour of every day should be the period during which you mass your energies, formulate your goals, and firm your resolve. If you use it well, you are on your way to a creative miracle.

How do you start?

You simplify, outlining the potential problems you will face. Cast out the trivial and the irrelevant from the treasure house of your mind.

When you chart your course, you must define your objectives so clearly that they are unmistakable.

But, above and beyond these practical concerns, you must energize your spirit with muscle and grit and sinew. You must prepare to take the plunge, get yourself ready to spring fearlessly from the diving board of your mind into the swimming pool of life.

Sit up in bed, throw off your bedsheets, rub the sleep from your eyes, and give yourself wise counsel. Tell yourself that you will be human toward yourself, forgetting the blunders of the past and living in the present. You must stop blaming yourself for your imperfections with the unfailing reminder that nobody is perfect. You must realize that you will have to become a friend to yourself before you can become a friend to others. You must understand that you reach success by climbing resolutely from the pit of failure.

While bathing, your pep talk should gain momentum. As the stream of water refreshes your body, you must freshen your soul. As the soap washes away the external dirt, you must cleanse yourself of the internal dirt of negative feelings.

Brushing your teeth, you should continue your thorough preparations for living a creative day. See in your mind the good successful moments of your life; bring them into focus so that they become part of you. Appreciate your image of yourself, even with its imperfections.

Now you get dressed and you still have time to mass your thinking for action. Don't squander your thoughts or pretend they are of no importance. Nothing is more important to your welfare than the quality of the thoughts and images filtering through your mind. Don't dilute their impact or let them career in all directions. Instead, tell yourself that happiness is your birthright and success is your prize. Stop shortchanging yourself; start living.

Your first hour is your hour of decision, Within its sixty-minute confines, you must make the decision as to whether you will charge forward toward your goals or crawl into a dark dungeon to fester. Remember you will not always win. Some days, the most resourceful individual will taste defeat. But there is, in this case, always tomorrow—after you have done your best to achieve success today.

Again, during this first hour, go back to the mirror to complete your physical preparations and—while brushing your hair or shaving or dabbing on lipstick—complete your emotional preparations. Straighten the seams of your self-image; build that smile of confidence.

Then eye your goals for creative living on this day—and move.

Please read this letter from a woman in Florida:

Dear Dr. Maltz:

On January 5, I had the privilege of hearing you at Broward Community College (Fort Lauderdale, Florida). You requested that I send you the following information:

Psycho-Cybernetics was first recommended to me by my neighbor. He is a midget and he stated that your book had made the difference between his personal success and failure in life. Until he read your book, he considered himself a failure, feeling that the whole world was against him. He said that *Psycho-Cybernetics* provided the technique for the personal victory and success he now enjoys.

He is comptroller for the chain of ———— Markets. I believe their main office is in Phoenix. He is affiliated with the organization known as the Little People of America and, if I remember correctly, was president of it. He is an outstanding member of Toastmasters International, and served as the president of the local chapter. His wife . . . is a midget and enjoys her life. . . . They have three adopted children, who are of normal size. . . . The children enjoyed a wonderful relationship with their adoptive parents.

Please accept the enclosure with the prayer that God will reveal to you His meaning in Hebrews 10: 22b: "Without shedding of blood is no remission."

Now read this second letter, from an accountant, which was sent to me all the way from Bombay, India:

It would be a sheer ingratitude on my part if I did not write to you about the great light your excellent book *Psycho-Cybernetics* has thrown into my mind about its own working. To say the least, you have revealed in your book through a Western mind, the Supreme Truth which has been and is being taught in the Hindu Religion since time immemorial, and what is most important to me is that this Supreme Truth has been revealed to me—or at least I have been able to understand it—a great deal more clearly through your book than I had ever done before.

It is not that I had not read the books of my religion before I read your book, and neither is it that I did not believe them. It was only that I simply did not understand how our minds and ourselves are two different things, the first controlling or being capable of controlling the other. This has been very excellently and patiently explained by you so kindly and has thrown a completely new and benevolent effect on my entire being. I am feeling greatly liberated. Your book, dear Doctor, is above psychoanalysis, which also I had tried not without advantage and other normal gimmicks, which are available cheaper by dozens.

To put it frankly, I am at a loss to find the words that can fully express how delighted I have been to read your book through and through, and how grateful I feel for what I received from it.

I have been strongly urging every one of my friends and acquaintances to read *Psycho-Cybernetics*, telling them that you have revealed the Supreme Truth which has been and is being taught by our own religion.

I wish you, Doctor, an ever-multiplying success in bringing peace and happiness to human beings and life generally everywhere. I would deem it a great favor to be able to call on you if you ever chance to visit India. Notwithstanding that, I do stand associated with you right now in mind and spirit.

> With great respect, I am,
> Yours truly,
> *Sudhir Mehta*

1. The first hour of the day is takeoff time, when you strain to move toward a creative day.

2. You remain alert for the first sign of negative feelings and prepare to sidetrack them and lunge toward productive living.

3. Every day you return to your big self.

4. When you encourage others, you encourage yourself.

5. Daily, your goal is to grow in stature as a human being.

6. Adjusting to pressure, yearning for improvement, your daily goal is Victory.

Principles to Live By

1. Creative living means trying. Camus, the great French philosopher, said that greatness means trying to be great. In the same way, success means trying to be successful.

2. Imagination is constructive with worthwhile goals and destructive with no goals.

3. Four principles of relaxation: forgive others; forgive yourself; see yourself at your best; keep up with yourself.

4. Happiness is internal.

5. The positive habit of confidence is as easy to master as the negative habit of frustration.

6. Accept your weaknesses and you cushion all shocks.

7. Compassion is the basis of morality, and compassion for self leads to compassion for others.

8. Unmask; stop pretending.

9. Live through your mistakes, not with them.

10. Never retire from life. You can't take your self-image, toss it in a satchel, go to the airport, check it in a locker, and throw the key away. Life won't let you.

11. Accept yourself as you are, *then* work to improve yourself.

12. You can be a winner. Athletes who reach 65 percent of their goals are champions. You can be a champion in the art of living, a professional human being, by remembering you can't reach all your goals. Reach 65 percent of them and you are a winner.

EXERCISE

Write the word "HOPE" on paper or mirror, then act out the following role as you soliloquize with yourself:

"What is hope? It is becoming. In these violent uncertain times, when many of us wonder what will become of the human race, remember that it depends on the individual and his desires.

"Socrates said 'Know thyself' and Marcus Aurelius said 'Be thyself' while Shakespeare said 'To thine own self be true.' My own statement must go beyond these passive statements to *action*. Every day I must adjust my self-image in keeping with changing conditions, moving toward goals even when asleep, because, asleep, my success mechanism is at work subconsciously.

"What am I doing? What am I becoming? Therein lies the hope of mankind—in what I, and millions of other people, are doing and becoming.

"So today is important. Today I will live creatively, dynamically, adding years to my life and life to my years. I will make today the best day of my life. And when tomorrow is today, I will repeat this promise. Until my life is creative and I am on my way to better status as a professional human being, I will not give up."

Thoughts to Live By

1. *God gave man two eyes to see the sunlight within him.* See this inner sunlight every day.

254

2. *When you hide from your creative self, you hide from God.* Stop hiding. You're not a criminal but a person looking to grow and achieve and become.

God Helps Those Who Help Themselves

In Birmingham, Alabama, recently, I lectured and afterward answered people's questions. During the question-and-answer period, I was asked this: "Don't you think if we start out each day first with God that we can't lose regardless of what comes?"

I answered that you must finish the day on your own, remembering that God helps those who help themselves.

Later, someone handed me this note:

A man bought an old run-down farm with weeds over his head. He worked it into a beautiful cultivated farm. The local minister came one day and said to him: "My, what you and God have done with this place!" The man said: "Yes, sir. You should have seen it when just God had it."

Remember, your creative day starts with you, with your first hour. You live one creative day, then another. Soon your life is creative. And that, in a nutshell, is what psycho-cybernetics is all about.

FOR MORE INFORMATION

On Psycho-Cybernetics
Workshops, Books, Films
And Cassette Tapes,
Call TOLL FREE:

800-528-0446

P.O. Box 1969, Scottsdale, AZ 85252